Time Together

THE **FAMILY** DEVOTIONAL

Time Together

THE **FAMILY** DEVOTIONAL

CWR

STEVE AND BEKAH LEGG

For our girls –

Amber, Emmie, Maddie, Gemma and Megan

Copyright © Steve and Bekah Legg 2017
Published 2018 by CWR, Waverley Abbey House, Waverley Lane, Farnham, Surrey
GU9 8EP, UK. Registered Charity No. 294387. Registered Limited Company No. 1990308.
Reprinted in 2018.
The right of Steve and Bekah Legg to be identified as the authors of this work has been
asserted by them in accordance with the Copyright, Designs and Patents Act 1988.
For a list of National Distributors visit www.cwr.org.uk/distributors
All Scripture references are from the Good News Bible (Anglicised © 2004) published
by The Bible Societies/Collins © American Bible Society. All rights reserved.
Every effort has been made to ensure that this book contains the correct permissions
and references, but if anything has been inadvertently overlooked the Publisher will be
pleased to make the necessary arrangements at the first opportunity. Please contact
the Publisher directly for further source information.
Concept development, editing, design and production by CWR.
Printed in the UK by Page Bros.
ISBN: 978-1-78259-798-8

Contents

Introduction

How do you feel about meeting new people?

In our family, we have five daughters; a couple of them are super shy, but the others love going out, exploring and meeting new people. Both my husband Steve and I do too. Wherever I go – whether I'm walking down the street or sitting on a train – I love talking to the people I meet, getting to know them a little, having a laugh together or even just sharing a smile. Steve talks to everyone too – he knows the names of all the checkout operators in our local supermarket, the guy who takes our takeaway orders and the people who walk on the beach where we take our dog, Colbie.

Over the years, we've met some really interesting people. Steve has travelled far and wide with his work and he's met comedians, politicians and TV celebrities. We've met people who have changed their communities, who have set up amazing projects and given up everything to take care of other people.

But in the middle of a world full of exciting people to meet, there remains one person who we still love to meet with the most – Jesus. The amazing thing about Jesus is that there is always more to know, always more to find out and perhaps more amazing still is the fact that *He* loves to meet with *us*.

Creating a bit of time in the day to meet with Jesus, to get to know Him a little better, to share a story and maybe a smile, is one of the most important things we can do. Time spent with Jesus makes any day better.

We live at a time in history when families are spending less and less time together, and even when we are in the same place we are often absorbed in different screens and activities. We are under increasing pressure to do more homework, overtime at work and even to do more at church. It's good to pause, to spend proper time together and to invite God to share that time with us.

It's why my family and I have written this 12-week devotional – to help you and your own family do just that. It's good to find time to be together, and this will look different for everyone. Breakfast may be a good time to get together for some, or maybe dinner or bedtime would work best for you? Our family has always found that the evenings are the easiest time to get together and talk about the things that matter, but that might just be because some of us are quite grumpy when we wake up!

So, we've written these devotional notes to help you and your family pause and meet with Jesus, as well as get to know some of the people who met Him before we did. Some of the characters we will encounter lived before Jesus was born, but they had amazing meetings with Jesus' Father God. Their stories tell us so much about who God is, how He loves His people and what that means for us today. People like Noah, Abraham and Ruth were very ordinary people, who God used in extraordinary ways to help Him change the world. It's exciting to think we can partner with Him like that too!

Over the years, I have come to realise how blessed I was to be brought up in a family who taught me how to find God in the pages of the Bible, and who showed me how wonderful it is to be able to meet with Jesus each day and share my life with Him. It's a gift I'm delighted to be able to share with my own children and with you.

Our prayer is that, over the next 12 weeks, you will grow closer together as a family and that you will discover new things about each other as you meet with Jesus and deepen your relationship with God. We pray that you'll know God's presence, not just as you read these devotions, but in the details of every day – and that this small season will develop into a lifetime of getting to know Jesus better, sharing your life with Him and following where He leads you.

Bekah

God sees the good...

Genesis 6:9–14

'This is the story of Noah. He had three sons, Shem, Ham, and Japheth. Noah had no faults and was the only good man of his time. He lived in fellowship with God, but everyone else was evil in God's sight, and violence had spread everywhere. God looked at the world and saw that it was evil, for the people were all living evil lives.

God said to Noah, "I have decided to put an end to the whole human race. I will destroy them completely, because the world is full of their violent deeds. Build a boat for yourself out of good timber; make rooms in it and cover it with tar inside and out.'

Something to think about

At the beginning of Noah's story we learn something about God that can make us feel a bit uncomfortable. Because God hates evil so much, He can't bear to let it carry on, so He decides to destroy the whole world to get rid of it. Frightening, hey? Nobody likes evil, but destroying the world seems a bit drastic – after all, we've all done things wrong.

But the great thing in this story is discovering that although God hates evil, He still looks for what is good, and He never allows His anger at the badness in the world to stop Him from noticing those who follow Him. He doesn't punish Noah and his family alongside the rest of humanity, which had become so evil, because even in the midst of all that was bad, they still followed God.

Bekah says...

When I was at school, I used to hate it when the teacher made the whole class stay in at break because a few people had been naughty – it always seemed really unfair. When I became a teacher I tried really hard not to do the same thing, and to notice when my students were behaving well.

Did you know?

It's easy to get lost in a crowd. It is estimated that there are over 7 billion people in the world, but God knows you and everything you do. He never loses sight of you!

Something to talk about

- Have you ever felt like you have been in trouble because of something someone else did?
- How did that make you feel?

Pray

God, thank You that even though there are billions of people in the world, You see me, You know me and You know what I do. Thank You that I'm never lost in the crowd with You. Amen.

Obedience to God

Genesis 7:1–5

'The LORD said to Noah, "Go into the boat with your whole family; I have found that you are the only one in all the world who does what is right. Take with you seven pairs of each kind of ritually clean animal, but only one pair of each kind of unclean animal. Take also seven pairs of each kind of bird. Do this so that every kind of animal and bird will be kept alive to reproduce again on the earth. Seven days from now I am going to send rain that will fall for forty days and nights, in order to destroy all the living beings that I have made." And Noah did everything that the LORD commanded.'

Something to think about

This is where things get really interesting. Imagine being Noah, with God asking you to build a huge boat in the middle of the countryside and then start collecting animal couples. It sounds like a crazy thing to do – people must have thought he was bonkers!

But Noah didn't ask God if He was joking, or if He'd gone mad: he just got on with the job. The Bible says that Noah did *everything* the Lord commanded. Noah's goodness and obedience proved that God was right to rescue him. Noah didn't question God, he just trusted Him and did what He said.

Bekah says...

Obedience sometimes seems a bit boring. And sometimes we don't like being told what to do - especially if it's something we don't want to do. But God doesn't give us commands for the sake of it or to be bossy: it's to take care of us and those around us - just the way He was taking care of Noah, his family and the animals in this story.

Steve says...

We have a beautiful dog called Colbie, and she is very obedient. It's really important that she does what we command - once she was about to run across the road in front of a car, but she stopped when I shouted at her and it saved her life!

Did you know?

Many experts think it would have taken Noah about 100 years to build the ark. That's a lot of obedience!

Something to talk about

· How good are you at following commands?
· Why do we sometimes do the opposite of what we're asked?

Pray

God, thank You for loving us. Help us to be quick to obey You when You ask us to do something. Amen.

Caring for God's world

Genesis 7:13–16

*'On that same day Noah and his wife went into the boat
with their three sons, Shem, Ham, and Japheth, and their
wives. With them went every kind of animal, domestic and
wild, large and small, and every kind of bird. A male and a
female of each kind of living being went into the boat with
Noah, as God had commanded. Then the LORD shut the
door behind Noah.'*

Something to think about

This is the second time in the Bible that God asks humans
to take care of animals. The first time was back in the
Garden of Eden when God asked Adam and Eve to take
care of the earth and everything in it. Now it's Noah's turn.
As we have read, Noah and his family are good, so God
doesn't want to punish them, and He doesn't want the
animals to suffer because of what people have done either.

Sometimes we can forget that animals, birds, fish and
even creepy crawlies were made by God, and that He was
pleased with what He made. Today, God still wants His
people to take care of His world and all the living things
in it. This means being kind to animals, thinking carefully
about where the food we eat comes from and learning how
our actions affect the earth. We need to protect the world
and make sure it doesn't suffer because of people's greed.

Bekah says...

I used to live in Africa, where there are some amazing animals! I think my favourites are elephants - they are so big, yet so clever and gentle. It makes me sad that so many people hunt them to sell their tusks for a lot of money. I have a friend who rescues baby elephants - it's an amazing job and is helping to make sure elephants don't become extinct.

Did you know?

We don't know exactly how many animals there were on the ark, but one expert thinks it could have held about 16,000 animals with enough room for all of them to sleep and eat!

Something to talk about

· What are your favourite animals?
· What could you do to help protect the world they live in?

Pray

Father God, thank You for the beautiful world You created for us to live in. Help us to take care of it and not spoil it. Amen.

The long wait

Genesis 8:1–5

'God had not forgotten Noah and all the animals with him in the boat; he caused a wind to blow, and the water started going down. The outlets of the water beneath the earth and the floodgates of the sky were closed. The rain stopped, and the water gradually went down for 150 days. On the seventeenth day of the seventh month the boat came to rest on a mountain in the Ararat range. The water kept going down, and on the first day of the tenth month the tops of the mountains appeared.'

Something to think about

Noah and his family were on that boat for almost a year before any sign of land started to reappear out of the water. Imagine that! Imagine the smell! Imagine taking care of all those animals, all day, every day and never knowing when you were going to get a day off! There wasn't even any exciting scenery out of the window – it was just water, everywhere you looked. It would have been easy to worry about what was going to happen. But God had it under control. He hadn't forgotten Noah and his family; He had a plan to give them a whole new life.

I don't know about you, but I haven't ever been stuck on a boat for months on end, but I have had hard times that seemed to go on and on like they would never end. Times when I've been tempted to wonder if God had forgotten me. This story helps us remember that with God, that never happens. He always sees where we are and what we're going through – and He always has a plan. Always.

Did you know?
Waiting for a baby can seem like forever – it takes 40 long weeks, or in the case of one of our daughters, 42! But that's nothing compared to an elephant's pregnancy, which lasts 95 weeks! That's almost two years. Imagine how long that would seem!

Something to talk about
· Have you ever had to wait a long time for a promise to come true?
· How did the wait feel?

Pray
Father God, thank You for never forgetting me. Thank You for always keeping Your promises. Please help me to wait patiently and trust You. Amen.

Grateful to God

Genesis 8:15–20

'God said to Noah, "Go out of the boat with your wife, your sons, and their wives. Take all the birds and animals out with you, so that they may reproduce and spread over all the earth." So Noah went out of the boat with his wife, his sons, and their wives. All the animals and birds went out of the boat in groups of their own kind. Noah built an altar to the Lord; he took one of each kind of ritually clean animal and bird, and burnt them whole as a sacrifice on the altar.'

Something to think about

Do you know what we love about this part of the story? It's that Noah's first thought when he gets off the boat is to thank God for taking care of him and his family. Most people would want to have a good look around, see where they were and if they recognised anything, check out this new land and see how it looked after such an almighty flood. But Noah lets all of those things wait. He knows the most important thing to do is to thank God for all He has done and celebrate what a great God He is! When exciting things happen, it's easy to forget what's important and who's important. Let's never forget to thank God for all He does for us.

Bekah says...

What are you like when you're given a present – for your birthday or at Christmas? Do you tear the wrapping off and start playing, or do you stop for a moment to say 'thank you' to the person who has given you the gift?

Did you know?

Archaeologists have spent years looking for the remains of Noah's ark, but many scientists think the ark would have been taken apart to use the wood to build with, so there's nothing left to be found.

Steve says...

Stop and think about who has been kind to you today. Is there someone you need to say 'thank you' to?

Something to talk about

· What's the best gift you've ever been given?
· What did you do when you were given it?

Pray

Father God, You are wonderful. You give us so many things. You take care of us and give us all we need. Thank You. Amen.

God's promise

Genesis 9:12–16

'As a sign of this everlasting covenant which I am making with you and with all living beings, I am putting my bow in the clouds. It will be the sign of my covenant with the world. Whenever I cover the sky with clouds and the rainbow appears, I will remember my promise to you and to all the animals that a flood will never again destroy all living beings. When the rainbow appears in the clouds, I will see it and remember the everlasting covenant between me and all living beings on earth.'

Something to think about

An everlasting covenant. What is that? A covenant is an old-fashioned word for a promise. A really, really serious promise. The Bible often tells us about God's covenants with His people – the promises He makes. This was a really important one. God promised that He would never flood the whole earth again.

And it was an everlasting covenant; a forever promise. God doesn't break His promises: we can trust that they are still true today, tomorrow and the days and years after that. God loves us. In another part of the Bible, God promises that He has plans to give us 'hope and a future' (Jer. 29:11). He plans to keep His promise to give us a world to live in and a life to live. And every time we see a rainbow, we can remember that.

Did you know?

The world's longest-lasting rainbow was seen over Sheffield, England on 14 March, 1994 – it lasted from 9am to 3pm. That's six whole hours!

Steve says...

When Bekah and I got married, we promised to love and take care of each other for the rest of our lives, and we wear wedding rings to remind us of that promise.

Something to talk about

· What promises have people made to you?
· How do you remember them?

Pray

Father God, thank You that You love us so much and You don't ever want to hurt us. Help us to remember that the promise You made to Noah is true for us too. Amen.

Something for the weekend

Why not visit a farm, zoo or go for a walk in the countryside and meet some of the animals God created?

The family

Genesis 11:27–31

'These are the descendants of Terah, who was the father of Abram, Nahor and Haran. Haran was the father of Lot, and Haran died in his native city, Ur in Babylonia, while his father was still living. Abram married Sarai, and Nahor married Milcah, the daughter of Haran, who was also the father of Iscah. Sarai was not able to have children. Terah took his son Abram, his grandson Lot, who was the son of Haran, and his daughter-in-law Sarai, Abram's wife, and with them he left the city of Ur in Babylonia to go to the land of Canaan. They went as far as Haran and settled there.'

Something to think about

We're starting a new story today, and it begins with a lot of complicated and different sounding names. We are going to be looking at some of these characters over the next few weeks, so it's good to get to know them. First, there's Abram and his wife Sarai. They have never been able to have children of their own, but for years they have helped to take care of their nephew Lot, whose dad had died. It's a close family and they've lived together for years.

There are lots of different types of families. Some of us live with our mum and dad, others live with just one parent and some of us live with other people who love and take care of us. But God planned for each of us to live and be loved within a family, no matter what form that family takes.

Bekah says...

Our family is different from some because we are a blended family. Two of the girls are mine and Steve is their step-dad, and three of the girls are Steve's and I'm their step-mum. And sometimes we have had other children live with us when their mum and dad couldn't take care of them. But really, we just think of them all as 'our' children, and we love them all the same. It's complicated, but we love our special family.

Something to talk about

- Who belongs in your family?
- Is there anyone else you take care of?

Pray

Dear God, thank You that You designed families to give us a place to be loved and looked after. Help us to always welcome others in, and to be grateful for those who love us. Amen.

A great promise

Genesis 12:1–3

'The Lord said to Abram, "Leave your country, your relatives and your father's home, and go to a land that I am going to show you. I will give you many descendants, and they will become a great nation. I will bless you and make your name famous, so that you will be a blessing.

I will bless those who bless you,
But I will curse those who curse you.
And through you I will bless all the nations."'

Something to think about

Wow! We looked at God's amazing promise to Noah last week, but this is an even more amazing promise for Abram. God promises to make Abram into a great nation – that means his children, his grandchildren and his great-grandchildren are going to be so many that they'll make a whole country of people! God says He will protect Abram, and that everyone is going to talk about how amazing Abram is, and the whole world will be blessed because of him! God's plan and promise for Abram is not just for Abram himself, but for the whole world.

What a fantastic promise! But what on earth does it all mean? How can it all happen? We're going to watch the story unfold over the next few weeks, but for now, let's remember that God always keeps His promise, even when it seems impossible.

Bekah says...

Abram believed that this promise would come true in the future for his descendants, even though he might not live to see it all happen. He knew that the choices he made would leave a legacy for generations to come. It's quite incredible to think that what we do with our lives could make a difference for centuries.

Steve says...

One of my favourite quotes comes from Martin Luther King, Jr: 'I have a dream that my four little children will one day live in a nation where they will not be judged by the colour of their skin, but by the content of their character.'

Something to talk about

· What difference would you like your life to make?
· How can you make sure your life is a blessing to others?

Pray

Father God, thank You that You love us and want good things for us. Help us to always share that love with others and be a blessing to those we meet. Amen.

Go!

Genesis 12:1,4–8

'The LORD said to Abram, "Leave your country, your relatives and your father's home, and go to a land that I am going to show you". When Abram was 75 years old, he started out from Haran, as the LORD had told him to do; and Lot went with him. Abram took his wife Sarai, his nephew Lot, and all the wealth and all the slaves they had acquired in Haran, and they started out for the land of Canaan. When they arrived in Canaan, Abram travelled through the land until he came to the sacred tree of Moreh, the holy place at Shechem. (At that time the Canaanites were still living in the land.) The LORD appeared to Abram and said to him, "This is the country that I am going to give to your descendants." Then Abram built an altar there to the LORD, who had appeared to him. After that, he moved on south to the hill country east of the city of Bethel and set up his camp between Bethel on the west and Ai on the east. There also he built an altar and worshipped the LORD.'

Something to think about

God gave Abram an amazing promise, but He also asked Abram to do something very hard. He asked him to leave his home, his parents and everyone he knew – and just go. God didn't even tell Abram where he was going. He just said He would tell him when they arrived. What a hard thing to do!

If you were Abram, wouldn't you want all the details of where you were going and what it would be like, to make sure it was worth leaving everything behind? We would! But Abram doesn't argue, worry or ask for more information. He just packs up his stuff, collects his wife, his nephew and his workers and sets out, waiting for God to tell him when to stop. How brave!

Did you know?

Abram's journey was a long one – he and his family travelled 1,000 miles before they reached the land God had promised them, and that was without planes, trains or even a car!

Something to talk about

· What's the longest journey you've ever been on?
· How much do you like travelling?

Pray

Dear Lord Jesus, help me to be obedient like Abram, to trust You when You ask me to do things, even when they're very hard and will take a long time. Amen.

Lies

Genesis 12:10–13

'But there was a famine in Canaan, and it was so bad that Abram went farther south to Egypt, to live there for a while. When he was about to cross the border into Egypt, he said to his wife Sarai, "You are a beautiful woman. When the Egyptians see you, they will assume that you are my wife, and so they will kill me and let you live. Tell them that you are my sister; then because of you they will let me live and treat me well."'

Something to think about

Not long after Abram and Sarai get to the land God had promised them, things get tough again: there was a famine! Abram takes the family to Egypt where they can find food and live for a while, but he worries about his beautiful wife. In fact, he worries about himself – he's worried the Egyptians will want to take his beautiful wife for themselves and that they might kill him in the process!

Abram has trusted God for such a long journey, but in this moment he forgets that God is in control and instead tries to come up with his own solution. He decides to go somewhere different and to lie to anyone they meet, pretending that Sarai is his sister and not his wife. It's hard to believe he's forgotten God's promise to protect him already!

Steve says...

Telling fibs is never a good idea. Sometimes it's tempting, sometimes it even seems as though it will make someone else happier: but it really matters that we tell the truth. Even when that's hard, even when we'll get in trouble, and sometimes, even when it will make someone else sad.

Did you know?

In John 14:6, Jesus describes Himself as 'the truth'. When we choose to follow Jesus, that means we try to be like Him... so that must include being truthful.

Something to talk about

· When have you wanted to tell a fib to avoid getting in trouble?
· What happened?

Pray

Dear Lord Jesus, thank You for being the truth. Thank You that we can always trust You, and that You are true to Your promises. Please give us the courage to be truthful, always. Amen.

WEEK 2:
A FAMILY AFFAIR
FRIDAY

Trouble

Genesis 12:14–20

'When [Abram] crossed the border into Egypt, the Egyptians did see that his wife was very beautiful. Some of the court officials saw her and told the king how beautiful she was, so she was taken into his palace. Because of her the king treated Abram well and gave him flocks of sheep and goats, cattle, donkeys, slaves, and camels. But because the king had taken Sarai, the LORD sent terrible diseases on him and on the people of his palace. Then the king sent for Abram and asked him, "What have you done to me? Why didn't you tell me that she was your wife? Why did you say that she was your sister, and let me take her as my wife? Here is your wife; take her and get out!" The king gave orders to his men, so they took Abram and put him out of the country, together with his wife and everything he owned.'

Something to think about

Abram had good reason to be worried about Sarai. Pharaoh, the king of Egypt, did think she was beautiful, and Abram's lie kept Abram safe. But it didn't keep Sarai safe; Pharaoh took her to be his wife, even though she was already married to Abram. What a mess!

Thankfully, God steps in to protect Sarai and her marriage to Abram, even though Abram hadn't trusted Him. God makes Pharaoh poorly, and warns Pharaoh that he can't have Sarai for a wife. Amazingly, Pharaoh gives Sarai back to Abram and sends them away with lots of money!

Bekah says...

I love that God takes care of us, even when we've tried to do things our way. It seems a little like Pharaoh got punished because of Abram's lie, but really God was stepping in to fix the mess that Abram, Sarai and Pharaoh had got themselves into.

Did you know?

In the Bible, Egypt seems to have been the place to run to in the bad times. Jacob's family find food in Egypt during another famine, and Mary and Joseph even took baby Jesus there to keep Him safe from an angry King Herod.

Something to talk about

- Have you ever got yourself into a mess that you couldn't fix by yourself?
- How did things get better?

Pray

Dear God, thank You for always knowing better than us. We're sorry for the times when we ignore You and get ourselves into trouble. Thank You for always helping us when we ask. Amen.

Too many sheep

Genesis 13:1–7

'Abram went north out of Egypt to the southern part of Canaan with his wife and everything he owned, and Lot went with him. Abram was a very rich man, with sheep, goats, and cattle, as well as silver and gold. Then he left there and moved from place to place going towards Bethel. He reached the place between Bethel and Ai where he had camped before and had built an altar. There he worshipped the LORD. Lot also had sheep, goats, and cattle, as well as his own family and servants. And so there was not enough pasture land for the two of them to stay together, because they had too many animals. So quarrels broke out between the men who took care of Abram's animals and those who took care of Lot's animals.'

Something to think about

Abram and his family have made it back to Canaan, the Promised Land, and even though Abram messed up in Egypt, God has been really good to him. They have lots of silver and gold and huge flocks and herds. In fact, they have so much that there's not really enough land for all the people and their animals. What a turn-around! In the last bit of the story there was a famine, but now God gives this family more than they know what to do with. But not everyone's happy – Abram's servants are arguing with Lot's servants about who will get the best land for their sheep.

Bekah says...

There are days, aren't there, when it feels like everyone should get on? Days like Christmas, when people have had presents, good food and all sorts of other treats. But the truth is that sometimes we don't stop to realise how fortunate we are, and we argue about things that don't really matter.

Did you know?

Sheep are mentioned in the Bible more than 500 times!

Something to talk about

· When are you most likely to fall out with someone?
· What helps you to stay kind?

Pray

Dear Lord God, help me to see the good things You give me and to focus on them. Sorry for the times I argue and am unkind to those around me. Amen.

Something for the weekend

Why not start creating your own family tree – what do you know about your ancestors?

Generous

Genesis 13:8–11

'Then Abram said to Lot, "We are relatives, and your men and my men shouldn't be quarrelling. So let's separate. Choose any part of the land you want. You go one way, and I'll go the other." Lot looked round and saw that the whole Jordan Valley, all the way to Zoar, had plenty of water, like the Garden of the LORD or like the land of Egypt. (This was before the LORD had destroyed the cities of Sodom and Gomorrah.) So Lot chose the whole Jordan Valley for himself and moved away toward the east. That is how the two men parted.'

Something to think about

Abram was a very generous man. He wasn't always perfect, and we've seen him make some bad decisions, but under it all he was kind. When he realises there isn't enough land for him and Lot to live together anymore, he suggests they split the land.

Abram knows God has promised to do amazing things for him, but that doesn't make him grab the best land; instead, he lets Lot choose where he would like to live and Abram takes what is left. It looks a lot like Abram is beginning to trust God again, not trying to make things work for himself.

Bekah says...

When I was a little girl, if I was sharing a bar of chocolate, the rule in my family was that whoever broke the bar in half didn't get to choose which side they kept. It was to make sure we didn't try to give ourselves more. But Abram went one better. He purposely let Lot take the best land. What a great sharer he was!

Steve says...

John 3:16 tells us that God loves us so much He gave us His only Son. That was super generous! God loves us to be just as kind and giving with the people in our lives.

Did you know?

According to a British newspaper, a man called Colin Harrison has been donating pints of blood every three months for 30 years. Over that time, he's given about 120 pints. It is thought that the blood he has donated has saved hundreds of thousands of lives, even babies with rare diseases.

Something to talk about

· How good are you at sharing?
· When has someone been very generous to you?

Pray

Dear God, thank You for everything You give me. Help me to freely and joyfully share all the gifts I have with the people around me. Amen.

Recognised and rewarded

Genesis 13:14–18

*'After Lot had left, the L*ᴏʀᴅ *said to Abram, "From where you are, look carefully in all directions. I am going to give you and your descendants all the land that you see, and it will be yours forever. I am going to give you so many descendants that no one will be able to count them all; it would be as easy to count all the specks of dust on earth! Now, go and look over the whole land, because I am going to give it all to you." So Abram moved his camp and settled near the sacred trees of Mamre at Hebron, and there he built an altar to the L*ᴏʀᴅ*.'*

Something to think about

Lot took the 'best' land, but Abram had made God very happy with his kindness to Lot. God rewarded Abram's generosity with His own incredible generosity, as He tells Abram that all the land he can see will belong to him. God also reminds Abram of His promise to give him and Sarai more descendants than they can even count!

Abram was so grateful to God, that he built an altar to celebrate all that God had done. The altar was a special place to give God a gift in return – which we call a sacrifice. It would stand there for years to remind Abram of how good God had been to him.

Bekah says...

We had a fright this year when one of our girls was very seriously ill. God was very good to us and we were able to see all the right doctors incredibly quickly, and before long, we were reassured that she would be OK. One of my friends bought us a plant, which I've put in the garden, to remind us of how good God was to us. Every time I look at it, I remember and I say 'Thank You' to God.

Did you know?

It'll make you happier if you say 'thank you' more. Every day, find something to thank someone else for. Give it a go. You will also find joy in making others happy!

Something to talk about

· When has God been very good to you?
· How do you make sure that you remember His goodness?

Pray

Dear God, You are so good. You love to give gifts that are even better than we can imagine! Thank You! Help us to give like You do. Amen.

A fair question

Genesis 15:1–6

'After this, Abram had a vision and heard the LORD say to him, "Do not be afraid, Abram. I will shield you from danger and give you a great reward." But Abram answered, "Sovereign LORD, what good will your reward do me, since I have no children? My only heir is Eliezer of Damascus. You have given me no children, and one of my slaves will inherit my property." Then he heard the LORD speaking to him again: "This slave Eliezer will not inherit your property; your own son will be your heir." The LORD took him outside and said, "Look at the sky and try to count the stars; you will have as many descendants as that." Abram put his trust in the LORD, and because of this the LORD was pleased with him and accepted him. Then the LORD said to him, "I am the LORD, who led you out of Ur in Babylonia, to give you this land as your own."'

Something to think about

Abram is getting older and older. And he's beginning to wonder just how God is going to keep His promise to give Abram more descendants than he can count. He wonders if maybe it will be his slave that inherits all his things. And he doesn't just think this in his head: he speaks it out loud to God.

It's amazing that we can ask God any question. It's OK to wonder how God will do something and to be a little uncertain when things seem impossible. Abram questions God about His promise, but he never forgets who he is talking to. Abram starts his prayer with 'Sovereign Lord' – that's like saying 'Supreme Ruler'. Abram starts his questions by admitting that God is in charge. When we do that, we can ask anything. Most importantly, Abram ends by trusting that God knows best.

Did you know?

With a good a pair of binoculars you can see 200,000 stars in the sky. And that's only a tiny fraction of how many are actually are out there!

Something to talk about

· What's the hardest question that you'd like to ask God?
· How do you start – and finish – your prayers to Him?

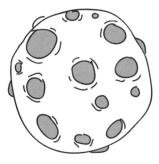

Pray

Father God, You *are* the supreme ruler of the universe! You created the sun, the moon, the sky and everything in it. It is amazing that I am allowed to talk to You. Thank You. Amen.

Man-made solutions

Genesis 16:1–2,5–6

'Abram's wife Sarai had not borne him any children. But she had an Egyptian slave woman named Hagar, and so she said to Abram, "The LORD has kept me from having children. Why don't you sleep with my slave? Perhaps she can have a child for me." Abram agreed with what Sarai said. Then Sarai said to Abram, "It's your fault that Hagar despises me. I myself gave her to you, and ever since she found out that she was pregnant, she has despised me. May the LORD judge which of us is right, you or me!" Abram answered, "Very well, she is your slave and under your control; do whatever you want with her." Then Sarai treated Hagar so cruelly that she ran away.'

Something to think about

Asking questions is one thing, but now Sarai is coming up with her own way of fixing the fact that she can't have children. She suggests Abram has a baby with her slave girl, Hagar, instead!

Yesterday, we saw Abram trusting that God knows best, but today, he and Sarai forget that lesson, as they try to work things out for themselves again. They get a baby – but it doesn't make them happy. In fact, Sarai is so jealous that she makes Hagar run away.

Bekah says...

When Sarai realised what a big mistake she had made, she was really upset, but instead of apologising to God and to Hagar, she just gets angry and is unkind to Hagar. Sometimes we do this too - we get cross with people around us when we've done something wrong, because we don't like admitting our mistakes.

Did you know?

Some Jewish scholars think that Hagar may have been Pharaoh's daughter, who travelled with Abram's family after she saw the miracle God carried out to rescue Sarai in Egypt.

Steve says...

Is there something you need to own up to? Saying sorry can make the situation a lot better.

Something to talk about

· What makes you grumpy?
· How good are you at admitting when you've made a mistake?

Pray

Father God, I'm sorry for the mistakes I make and for the times I choose to do bad things. Please help me to trust You and to make good decisions. Amen.

Never forgotten

Genesis 16:7–11

'The angel of the LORD met Hagar at a spring in the desert on the road to Shur and said, "Hagar, slave of Sarai, where have you come from and where are you going?" She answered, "I am running away from my mistress." He said, "Go back to her and be her slave." Then he said, "I will give you so many descendants that no one will be able to count them. You are going to have a son, and you will name him Ishmael, because the LORD has heard your cry of distress."'

Something to think about

Poor Hagar had become so miserable living with Sarai that she ran away. But she couldn't run from God. Hagar wasn't meant to be the answer to God's promise for Abram, but God doesn't blame her for what has happened. Instead, He blesses her and promises that, despite the loneliness she must have felt at that moment, she will have a son and a large family because God has seen her sadness.

God even tells Hagar what to call her son – Ishmael. It means 'God hears'. It's good to know that no matter where we are, or how alone we feel, God can hear our prayers for help. It's never too late, or too dark, or too difficult for God. He is the God who hears Hagar and me and you.

Steve says...

King David knew that God was always with him too.
He wrote this in Psalm 139:7-10:
'Where could I go to escape from you?
Where could I get away from your presence?
If I went up to heaven, you would be there;
if I lay down in the world of the dead, you
would be there.
If I flew away beyond the east
or lived in the farthest place in the west,
you would be there to lead me,
you would be there to help me.'

Did you know?

Your ears work even faster than your mouth! Most people can listen to around 450 words per minute.

Something to talk about

· Have you ever felt all alone with a problem?
· How does it feel to know that God is always listening, and always wants to help you?

Pray

Father God, thank You that there is nowhere I can go that You aren't with me, and that You always hear even my deepest thoughts. Amen.

What's in a name?

Genesis 17:3–5,15–16

'God said, "I make this covenant with you: I promise that you will be the ancestor of many nations. Your name will no longer be Abram, but Abraham, because I am making you the ancestor of many nations. You must no longer call your wife Sarai; from now on her name is Sarah. I will bless her, and I will give you a son by her. I will bless her, and she will become the mother of nations, and there will be kings among her descendants."'

Something to think about

Thirteen years have passed since Ishmael was born. Abram is now 99 years old. That's *old*! And yet, God promises once again that Abram *will* be the father of many nations and Sarai will be the mother. It's the third time God has turned up and made this promise, but this time it's a bit different: this time it's as if everything is going to change – and the changes start with their names.

Abram's name is changed to Abraham, which means 'father of many nations', and Sarai's name changes to Sarah, which means 'princess'. They have been given new names – new identities – to prepare them for what is about to happen. The promise is about to be fulfilled, and Sarah is included in it all...

Bekah says...

My full name is Rebekah. I used to think that my name meant 'princess', but actually it's a Hebrew name that means 'to tie up'. I think I preferred princess!

Did you know?

Some people choose some very interesting names for their children. Rock musician Frank Zappa called his children Moon Unit, Dweezil, Ahmet and Diva Muffin.

Steve says...

My full name is Stephen, and although I do not like to be called that, the meaning – 'crown' – is, in my opinion, very fitting!

Something to talk about

· Do you know what your name means?
· Why were you given that name?

Pray

Father God, thank You for knowing my name and having a wonderful plan for my life. Help me to follow You all my days. Amen.

Something for the weekend

Create a poster of God's promises for your family. You could choose some of your favourite Bible verses and write them out in your best handwriting, or paint some pictures to represent them.

A warm welcome

Genesis 18:1–5

'The LORD appeared to Abraham at the sacred trees of Mamre. As Abraham was sitting at the entrance of his tent during the hottest part of the day, he looked up and saw three men standing there. As soon as he saw them, he ran out to meet them. Bowing down with his face touching the ground, he said, "Sirs, please do not pass by my home without stopping; I am here to serve you. Let me bring some water for you to wash your feet; you can rest here beneath this tree. I will also bring a bit of food; it will give you strength to continue your journey. You have honoured me by coming to my home, so let me serve you." They replied, "Thank you; we accept."'

Something to think about

Abraham was a hospitable man. That means he was a man who gave visitors a warm welcome. Even strangers. When we read this part of the story, we know that the Lord was visiting Abraham, but Abraham didn't know that – he just saw three men. But he was a kind and generous man who offered food and drink to some hot and dusty passers-by; he even brought water to wash their feet.

It's easy to be hospitable to our friends – being kind to strangers takes more effort. But all through the Bible, God tells His people to take care of strangers and people who are left out. When we speak to someone who looks lonely, when we invite someone new to dinner, when we invite someone to play with us who is being left out, we're actually being just like Jesus. He went out of His way to speak to people no one else would.

Did you know?
One in ten people over the age 70 only see friends and family once a month. Would this make you feel lonely?

Something to talk about
· When has someone shown you a really warm and unexpected welcome?
· How good are you at including other people?

Steve says...
Why don't you invite someone different to your house or out to play, and show the kind of hospitality that Abraham did in this story?

Pray
Dear Lord Jesus, thank You for Your kindness in including everyone. Help me to be like You. Give me the courage to overcome my shyness or awkwardness, so that I can show love to lonely people. Amen.

Laughing at God

Genesis 18:8–14

'He took some cream, some milk, and the meat, and set the food before the men. There under the tree he served them himself, and they ate. Then they asked him, "Where is your wife Sarah?"

*"She is there in the tent," he answered. One of them said, "Nine months from now I will come back, and your wife Sarah will have a son." Sarah was behind him, at the door of the tent, listening. Abraham and Sarah were very old, and Sarah had stopped having her monthly periods. So Sarah laughed to herself...Then the L*ᴏʀᴅ *asked Abraham, "Why did Sarah laugh and say, 'Can I really have a child when I am so old?' Is anything too hard for the L*ᴏʀᴅ*? As I said, nine months from now I will return, and Sarah will have a son."'*

Something to think about

Sarah laughed when she heard God say that she would have a baby. She thought she was way too old. She thought she knew best – again! She thought it was impossible. But here's the thing: *nothing* is impossible for God, and sometimes He loves to do seemingly crazy things that no one expects or thinks possible, so that people can see Him at work. If Sarah really could have a baby in her old age, it would be the most amazing gift for Sarah, but it would also be the biggest news in town; everyone would talk about how great God is.

Bekah says...

Sometimes we don't expect God to do amazing things for us, but this story reminds us that God can do anything. Let's always be ready to ask God for crazy-big miracles and see what He will do.

Did you know?

According to a British newspaper, the oldest woman in the UK (and possibly the world!) to give birth naturally was Dawn Brooke in 1997. She was 59.

Something to talk about

· What is the most amazing thing God has done for you?
· How did that make you feel about God?

Steve says...

Is there something you haven't dared to ask God for, something really important and impossible? Why not ask Him now?

Pray

Dear Lord God, You are the most amazing God, and sometimes we forget just how awesome and powerful You are. Please show us Your power today. Amen.

Promise fulfilled

Genesis 21:1–7

'The LORD blessed Sarah, as he had promised, and she became pregnant and bore a son to Abraham when he was old. The boy was born at the time God had said he would be born. Abraham named him Isaac, and when Isaac was eight days old, Abraham circumcised him, as God had commanded. Abraham was a hundred years old when Isaac was born. Sarah said, "God has brought me joy and laughter. Everyone who hears about it will laugh with me." Then she added, "Who would have said to Abraham that Sarah would nurse children? Yet I have borne him a son in his old age."'

Something to think about

God really can do anything and He always keeps His promises. When she finally has her baby, Sarah laughs again, but this time with joy. God has given her the most amazing and unexpected gift, even though she tried to do things her way, even though she often forgot to trust Him, even though she made big mistakes. God's love and God's plan is bigger than Sarah's worries and problems and mistakes. Sarah finally learns to trust God, and that when she focuses on Him and His promises, her worries and problems don't feel so big.

God's love and plan for us is bigger than our worries and problems too. He loves to bring us joy, even when we think that is impossible. When our world seems too hard, and our problems too big, we need to focus on God and His promise to love and take care of us – so that we can find joy, just like Sarah.

Bekah says...

God says that He has plans to give us hope and a future (Jer. 29:11). That's a promise to focus on, when our world feels like it's all going wrong.

Steve says...

When I was a kid, I used to love watching the A-team TV series. Against all the odds, no matter how impossible it seemed, the A-team's plan always came together to bring a happy ending. One of the character's had the catchphrase – 'I love it when a plan comes together'.

Something to talk about

· When have you had to trust God to be bigger than your problems?
· How do you find joy when times are hard?

Pray

Father God, thank You that You are a Father who loves to bring us joy, a Father who loves to give us good things. Help us to remember this when we are frightened or angry or sad. Amen.

Testing

Genesis 22:1–5

'Some time later God tested Abraham; he called to him, "Abraham!" And Abraham answered, "Yes, here I am!" "Take your son," God said, "your only son, Isaac, whom you love so much, and go to the land of Moriah. There on a mountain that I will show you, offer him as a sacrifice to me." Early the next morning Abraham cut some wood for the sacrifice, loaded his donkey, and took Isaac and two servants with him. They started out for the place that God had told him about. On the third day Abraham saw the place in the distance. Then he said to the servants, "Stay here with the donkey. The boy and I will go over there and worship, and then we will come back to you."'

Something to think about

Isaac was an incredibly special boy. Every child is special, but Abraham and Sarah had waited such a long time for him to come and they loved him so much. This part of the story is hard to understand, as God asks Abraham to do the most unimaginable, impossible thing. He asks Abraham to give up his precious son Isaac, to place him on an altar and give him to God. What a bizarre and scary thing to ask Abraham to do!

But Abraham has learned a lot about God: he has learned to trust God no matter what happens. He knows God *gave* him Isaac, he knows God has promised him that *through* Isaac he would have more descendants than there are stars in the sky, and he knows that God is *good*. So, Abraham obeys God and sets out for the mountain with Isaac, trusting God to know and do what is best. Wow.

Steve says...

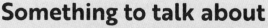

Obeying God isn't always easy: sometimes it means giving up things that we really love. I was very proud of our girls when they gave up some of their pocket money to help sponsor a little girl in Haiti and enable her to go to school.

Something to talk about

· Have you had to give up something you really wanted for God?
· What would you find hard to give up?

Pray

Father God, You are so important to me, I don't want to have anything in my life that becomes more important. I want to follow You all my life, no matter what You ask of me. Amen.

Provision

Genesis 22:7–14

'Isaac asked, "I see that you have the coals and the wood, but where is the lamb for the sacrifice?"

Abraham answered, "God himself will provide one." And the two of them walked on together. When they came to the place which God had told him about, Abraham built an altar and arranged the wood on it. He tied up his son and placed him on the altar, on top of the wood. Then he picked up the knife to kill him. But the angel of the LORD called to him from heaven, "Abraham, Abraham!"

He answered, "Yes, here I am." "Don't hurt the boy or do anything to him," he said. "Now I know that you honour and obey God, because you have not kept back your only son from him." Abraham looked round and saw a ram caught in a bush by its horns. He went and got it and offered it as a burnt offering instead of his son. Abraham named that place "The LORD Provides". And even today people say, "On the LORD's mountain he provides."'

Something to think about

Abraham really was willing to do anything for God. But God is a good God, and He never really wanted Abraham to kill his precious son. He just wanted to know that no matter how much Abraham loved Isaac, he still loved God more. So God showed up – He sent an angel and provided a sheep to be sacrificed instead.

This must have been such a hard test for Abraham, but because he was obedient he saw once again how amazing God is. He met another angel and he was able to tell the story of how God provided, to everyone he met.

Did you know?

Mount Moriah is still a very special place where people remember how God provides. King Solomon built a huge temple there and the Bible says that one day a temple will be built there again.

Something to talk about

· When has God provided for you in an amazing way?
· How did that change you?

Bekah says...

Sometimes God uses us to provide for other people - why not give some food to your local foodbank to help provide for a family who needs help?

Pray

Father God, You are a God who provides what we need. Thank You. Help me to always trust You, and be obedient to You. Amen.

WEEK 4:
A SPECIAL SON

WEEKEND

Be a blessing

Genesis 22:15–18

'The angel of the LORD called to Abraham from heaven a second time, "I make a vow by my own name – the LORD is speaking – that I will richly bless you. Because you did this and did not keep back your only son from me, I promise that I will give you as many descendants as there are stars in the sky or grains of sand along the seashore. Your descendants will conquer their enemies. All the nations will ask me to bless them as I have blessed your descendants – all because you obeyed my command." Abraham went back to his servants, and they went together to Beersheba, where Abraham settled.'

Something to think about

God loves how obedient Abraham has been. Over the years, Abraham has grown in his faith and learned to follow and trust God with everything. So God rewards Abraham with a promise that is not just for him, but for his children and his children's children and forever.

But there is something more in today's Bible passage – Abraham's descendants are going to bless the rest of the world. They are not to keep the blessing all for themselves; God wants them to live lives that show the rest of the world how wonderful God is, so that other people want to get to know Him too.

Bekah says...

God wants us to live lives like that too. God wants to give us great things so that we can share His love with everyone around us, and so that people will want to know who our wonderful God is.

Did you know?

A group of researchers at the University of Hawaii have estimated there are seven quintillion, five hundred quadrillion grains of sand in the world. We didn't even know those numbers existed!

Something to talk about

· What makes you want to know more about God?
· How do you show God's love to the people around you?

Pray

Father God, thank You for the people who have led me to get to know You. Help me to be someone who shares Your love with everyone I meet. Amen.

Something for the weekend

Why not have a big sort-out of some of your stuff this weekend, and see if there are things that you could give away to people who need it more than you?

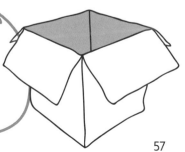

One thing after another

Ruth 1:1–6,19–21

'Long ago, in the days before Israel had a king, there was a famine in the land. So a man named Elimelech, who belonged to the clan of Ephrath and who lived in Bethlehem in Judah, went with his wife Naomi and their two sons Mahlon and Chilion to live for a while in the country of Moab. While they were living there, Elimelech died, and Naomi was left alone with her two sons, who married Moabite women, Orpah and Ruth. About ten years later Mahlon and Chilion also died, and Naomi was left all alone, without husband or sons. Some time later Naomi heard that the LORD had blessed his people by giving them a good harvest; so she got ready to leave Moab with her daughters-in-law.

When they arrived, the whole town got excited, and the women there exclaimed, "Is this really Naomi?""Don't call me Naomi," she answered; "call me Marah, because Almighty God has made my life bitter. When I left here, I had plenty, but the LORD has brought me back without a thing. Why call me Naomi when the LORD Almighty has condemned me and sent me trouble?"'

Something to think about

Naomi's life seems to go from bad to worse. First her family have to leave their home and go to a foreign country because the crops haven't grown in Israel, then her husband and even her children die. It's hard to imagine just how sad and lost she must have felt.

When she gets home to Bethlehem, she even changes her name to show just how sad and lonely she is. She thinks it's God's fault, and feels that He has forgotten her.

Bekah says...

Sometimes our lives feel like one sad thing after another, and it's easy to think God has forgotten us, just like Naomi felt. This week, we're going to look at how God was still there in the middle of Naomi's struggles, so that we can also find Him in the middle of our own tough times.

Something to talk about

· Has there been a time in your life when it felt like everything was going wrong?
· How did that make you feel about God?

Pray

Father God, thank You for giving us stories like Naomi's in the Bible, so that we can know that other people have gone through tough stuff too. And thank You that You are always there, in the middle of their struggles, and ours. Amen.

A good friend

Ruth 1:15–17

'So Naomi said to her, "Ruth, your sister-in-law has gone back to her people and to her god. Go back home with her." But Ruth answered, "Don't ask me to leave you! Let me go with you. Wherever you go, I will go; wherever you live, I will live. Your people will be my people, and your God will be my God. Wherever you die, I will die, and that is where I will be buried. May the LORD's worst punishment come upon me if I let anything but death separate me from you!"'

Something to think about

When Naomi returned to Bethlehem, she told her old friends that she had come home with nothing in her hands. But that wasn't quite true. She had told her daughters-in-law to turn around and stay in Moab, and Orpah did. Ruth however, refused. In fact, Ruth promised to never leave her – not ever. So, Naomi came home with an amazingly kind and loyal daughter-in-law.

Sometimes, when times are hard, it's easy to focus on what is going wrong in our lives and to forget the good things that God has given us. God didn't miraculously heal Naomi's family, and He didn't send an angel or speak out of a burning bush. But He did give Naomi a great friend in Ruth, and she was a real gift. On days when it feels like everything is going wrong, it's good to stop and look for the good; to see the gifts that God *has* given us.

Bekah says...

Back when I was a single mum with two little girls, things were really tough, but I had a best friend who stuck with me through everything. I always knew she would be there for me.

Did you know?

Ruth's promise to Naomi is often read by couples at weddings because it is such a fantastic promise to stick together.

Something to talk about

· Who has been a really great friend to you?
· What difference did that make?

Steve says...

Why not look back over your day today... Have you missed seeing something good that has happened?

Pray

Dear Lord Jesus, thank You for always being there, taking care of us even when we don't notice. Help us to see the gifts You give us and to remember that You're always here. Amen.

It just so happened..

Ruth 2:1–3

'Naomi had a relative named Boaz, a rich and influential man who belonged to the family of her husband Elimelech. One day Ruth said to Naomi, "Let me go to the fields to gather the corn that the harvest workers leave. I am sure to find someone who will let me work with him."

Naomi answered, "Go ahead, my daughter." So Ruth went out to the fields and walked behind the workers, picking up the corn which they left. It so happened that she was in a field that belonged to Boaz.'

Something to think about

Don't you love the story of Ruth? There are no amazing miracles, but there are lots of 'it so happened' moments (Ruth 2:3–4; 4:1). It's easy not to realise when God is at work: often we think something is an interesting coincidence or 'lucky timing', when actually God has been working in our lives to make things happen for our good. Of all the fields around Bethlehem, Ruth chooses to work in one that turns out to be the property of one of Naomi's relatives, and then he just so happens to come and visit as she's collecting corn.

Ruth and Naomi's life is hard, but God is working behind the scenes with a plan that will change everything, and this 'chance' meeting of Ruth and Boaz is just the beginning. He's a clever God!

Steve says...

Bekah and I lived at different ends of the country before we knew each other. But we just so happened to be on holiday in exactly the same place at exactly the same time in May 2007. That 'chance meeting' was just the beginning of another of God's great plans and I'm very grateful for that!

Did you know?

In 1930, a baby fell out of a window and a man called Joseph Figlock, who was walking by, caught it. A year later, the same infant fell from the same window and Joseph Figlock was walking underneath and caught him again!

Something to talk about

· What's the most amazing coincidence that has happened to you?
· Has God brought someone into your life at just the right time?

Pray

Father God, help me to see Your hand at work in my life and not to mistakenly think everything just happens by accident. Help me not to miss what You're doing. Amen.

Going the extra mile

Ruth 2:14–16, 20

'At mealtime Boaz said to Ruth, "Come and have a piece of bread, and dip it in the sauce." So she sat with the workers, and Boaz passed some roasted grain to her. She ate until she was satisfied, and she still had some food left over. After she had left to go on picking up corn, Boaz ordered the workers, "Let her pick it up even where the bundles are lying, and don't say anything to stop her. Besides that, pull out some corn from the bundles and leave it for her to pick up." "May the LORD bless Boaz!" Naomi exclaimed. "The LORD always keeps his promises to the living and the dead."'

Something to think about

Naomi is beginning to realise that God hasn't forgotten her at all. In fact, she's beginning to see that God is taking very good care of her and Ruth. One of the rules God gave His people was to allow widows and foreigners to collect leftover wheat and corn from the fields at harvest time. That's what Ruth was doing in the fields – picking up the grains the workers had dropped. But Boaz goes further: he tells his men to drop extra corn, and he invites Ruth to eat with him and his workers.

Naomi can see the heart of God working through Boaz – a man who knows that God loves to look after those who are struggling, and so he gives more than is required by God's law and more than Ruth can even eat... even though she is a widow from a foreign land.

Bekah says...

John 3:16 says that God so loved the world He sent His only son to die to save us. No one made God do that - He chose to, because He loves us so much. God loves it when we love people the way He does - extravagantly! How can you show God's love by being extra kind to someone?

Steve says...

Once when I was away on tour, my local Indian takeaway became worried about me as I hadn't ordered anything for a few weeks, so they called me to ask if I was OK! They also sent me a free 'welcome back' dhansak curry on my return. And very tasty it was, too!

Something to talk about

· When has someone 'gone the extra mile' for you?
· How did that make you feel?

Pray

Father God, thank You that there is nothing You wouldn't do for me. Help me to always be generous to those You bring across my path. Amen.

God is in the detail

Ruth 2:20; 3:6–7,9–13

'[Naomi] went on, "That man is a close relative of ours, one of those responsible for taking care of us." So Ruth went to the threshing place and did just what her mother-in-law had told her. When Boaz had finished eating and drinking, he was in a good mood. He went to the pile of barley and lay down to sleep. Ruth slipped over quietly, lifted the covers and lay down at his feet.

"Who are you?" he asked.

"It's Ruth, sir," she answered.

"The LORD bless you," he said. "Now don't worry, Ruth. I will do everything you ask; as everyone in town knows, you are a fine woman. It is true that I am a close relative and am responsible for you... I swear by the living LORD that I will take the responsibility."'

Something to think about

This is where the story starts to involve some creeping around in the dark! But the details behind the whispered conversations show us that God has been at work for years before this moment, creating plans to take care of Naomi and Ruth, and others like them who are struggling in poverty.

Just like the laws saying that people can collect the dropped grain, God had instructed His people to take responsibility for their family when someone becomes so poor they have to sell their land or even themselves.

That person was called a 'kinsman-redeemer', and they were obliged to buy things back for their relatives. Boaz is Naomi and Ruth's kinsman-redeemer: it's up to him to help them get back on their feet.

Steve says...

Centuries later, Jesus came to buy us back from the mistakes we make, mistakes that separate us from God. When He died on the cross, He paid the price that we should pay so that we could be close to God forever. Isn't that incredible?

Bekah says...

During a school trip, one of our girls wanted to buy a teddy bear, but when she got to the till, she realised she didn't have enough money. A lady behind her in the queue paid the extra – which meant Meg got something she couldn't really afford!

Something to talk about
· Has anyone ever helped you get out of a tricky situation?
· When have you helped someone else?

Pray
Lord Jesus, thank You for paying the price for my mistakes, so that I could come to know You – even though I don't deserve it. Thank You for loving me that much. Amen.

God is in the future

Ruth 4:13–17

*'So Boaz took Ruth home as his wife. The L*ORD* blessed her, and she became pregnant and had a son. The women said to Naomi, "Praise the L*ORD*! He has given you a grandson today to take care of you. May the boy become famous in Israel! Your daughter-in-law loves you, and has done more for you than seven sons. And now she has given you a grandson, who will bring new life to you and give you security in your old age." Naomi took the child, held him close, and took care of him. The women of the neighbourhood named the boy Obed. They told everyone, "A son has been born to Naomi!" Obed became the father of Jesse, who was the father of David.'*

Something to think about

This story has a happy ending – the whole neighbourhood could see that Naomi, who came home so sad and so bitter, was now full of joy. Ruth got married and had a child, Obed, and that seems like a happy enough ending. But there is something else in this story – a part of God's bigger plan – that Naomi and Ruth may never have lived to see. Ruth, this lady from a foreign, enemy land, becomes the great-grandma to King David, the greatest king Israel ever had. What an amazing honour! God can use *everyone*, no matter who we are or where we come from. In fact, it gets even better – in Matthew 1:6 we see that even further down Ruth's family tree is Jesus! Now that really is an honour!

Bekah says...

Often, we can only see what is happening right here, right now – but God always has a bigger plan. It can be hard to do, but we need to trust that God knows what He's doing (whether we can see it or not).

Did you know?

The actor Johnny Depp (aka Captain Jack Sparrow!) is the 20th cousin of Queen Elizabeth II.

Something to talk about

- Have you ever seen a sad part of your life turn out for the good?
- What helps you to keep on trusting God when things are difficult?

Pray

Dear Lord Jesus, I'm so glad that You are bigger and more wonderful than I could ever imagine. Help me to remember that You are in control even when I'm not. Amen.

Something for the weekend

Why don't you try finding something hidden this weekend? Take it in turns to hide treats and see who can find them first.

A frightening mission

1 Samuel 16:1–3

'The Lᴏʀᴅ said to Samuel, "How long will you go on grieving over Saul? I have rejected him as king of Israel. But now get some olive oil and go to Bethlehem, to a man named Jesse, because I have chosen one of his sons to be king."

"How can I do that?" Samuel asked. "If Saul hears about it, he will kill me!"

The Lᴏʀᴅ answered, "Take a calf with you and say that you are there to offer a sacrifice to the Lᴏʀᴅ. Invite Jesse to the sacrifice, and I will tell you what to do. You will anoint as king the man I tell you to."'

Something to think about

Israel was God's kingdom and it was being ruled by King Saul, but Saul had stopped following God and wasn't ruling Israel well. Samuel was God's prophet, which meant he was God's messenger. He was brilliant at hearing God's voice and telling people what God was saying to them.

It was an amazing privilege to be able to take God's messages to people, but on this day it was a rather frightening privilege. God had asked Samuel to go and find the next king and to tell him that he had been chosen by God – and it's not going to be Saul's son. Saul is not going to be happy if he finds out. Not happy at all. And that puts Samuel in a lot of danger. This mission God has for him is super important, but super dangerous.

Bekah says...

It's always amazing to have a mission from God, but it can be a little scary too. God's mission for us is to tell other people about Jesus. It's the most important thing we can ever do.

Did you know?

The Christian missionary Brother Andrew is an incredible man who has spent most of his life smuggling Bibles into countries where it is against the law to own one. He has often risked his life to do it. Now *that's* a dangerous mission!

Something to talk about

- What's the scariest thing you've done for God?
- How did you feel afterward?

Steve says...

It's time to go on a mission! Who could you tell about Jesus, or invite to church today?

Pray

Father God, it's amazing that You would ask me to go on a mission for You. Help me to have the courage to say 'Yes!' Amen.

Listening to God

1 Samuel 16:6–11

'When they arrived, Samuel saw Jesse's son Eliab and said to himself, "This man standing here in the Lord's presence is surely the one he has chosen." But the Lord said to him, "Pay no attention to how tall and handsome he is. I have rejected him, because I do not judge as people judge. They look at the outward appearance, but I look at the heart."

Then Jesse called his son Abinadab and brought him to Samuel. But Samuel said, "No, the Lord hasn't chosen him either." Jesse then brought Shammah. "No, the Lord hasn't chosen him either," Samuel said. In this way Jesse brought seven of his sons to Samuel. And Samuel said to him, "No, the Lord hasn't chosen any of these." Then he asked him, "Have you any more sons?"'

Something to think about

Samuel is scared, but he says 'yes' to God and goes to find God's next king. He visits the town of Bethlehem and goes to the home of Jesse, just as God asked him to. Jesse brings out his sons for Samuel to meet and they are big, tall, strong men who Samuel thinks look just perfect to be king.

But Samuel doesn't make a decision based on what *he* can see – he keeps listening to God. And God sees more than Samuel.

When we're making decisions about anything, it's important we stop and listen to God, because He always sees more than us. Sometimes we can think we know everything, and that the best thing to do is obvious, but God might have something even better in mind. We won't know unless we stop and ask Him.

Bekah says...

A friend of mine taught me never to say 'yes' straight away when someone asks me to do something important, but to always ask if I can have time to pray about it. It was good advice: if they can't wait, then I say 'no'. I've learned it's always best to get God's advice before making a big decision.

Did you know?

Everyone thinks bats have the best hearing, but actually scientists have discovered that moths are even better! They can hear a higher frequency than bats, which allows them to escape danger.

Something to talk about

· What are some of the hardest decisions you've had to make?
· Who did you go to for help?

Pray

God, thank You that You care about every decision I make. Help me to seek Your advice and listen to Your answer. Amen.

The boy king

1 Samuel 16:11–13

'Jesse answered, "There is still the youngest, but he is out taking care of the sheep."

"Tell him to come here," Samuel said. "We won't offer the sacrifice until he comes." So Jesse sent for him. He was a handsome, healthy young man, and his eyes sparkled. The LORD said to Samuel, "This is the one — anoint him!" Samuel took the olive oil and anointed David in front of his brothers. Immediately the Spirit of the LORD took control of David and was with him from that day on. Then Samuel returned to Ramah.'

Something to think about

I love how God often surprises us with His plan. It was the youngest boy in the family that He chose to be the next king. David was so young and 'unimportant' that his dad hadn't even bothered to bring him to meet Samuel. Time and again in the Bible, God uses the most unlikely people; the 'weaklings', the outsiders, the foreigners and the rejects.

No one is useless to God. *No one* is too young, weird or stupid in God's eyes. He has a wonderful plan for *everyone* and when He works with unlikely people, it shows the world two things. It shows the world that everyone matters and is valuable, and it shows just how amazing God is when He makes impossible things happen through people who couldn't do it on their own.

Steve says...

Years ago, God asked me to make a Christmas cartoon called 'It's a Boy' to give to schools - and it would cost a lot of money. There were only two problems: I didn't have the money and I didn't know how to make cartoons... pretty major weaknesses! But I prayed and asked God to provide what I needed. Over the next few years, I was given £250,000 and met people who could make cartoons. God is amazing!

Did you know?

Paul, one of the great leaders of the Church, said that he loved to boast about his weaknesses so that God's power could be more obvious working in him.

Something to talk about

· What are your weaknesses?
· How have you seen God work through them?

Pray

Father God, thank You for loving me despite my weaknesses and failures. Thank You for working through me anyway and letting me see Your amazing power. Amen.

The apprentice

1 Samuel 16:19–23

'So Saul sent messengers to Jesse to say, "Send me your son David, the one who takes care of the sheep." Jesse sent David to Saul with a young goat, a donkey loaded with bread, and a leather bag full of wine. David came to Saul and entered his service. Saul liked him very much and chose him as the man to carry his weapons. Then Saul sent a message to Jesse: "I like David. Let him stay here in my service." From then on, whenever the evil spirit sent by God came on Saul, David would get his harp and play it. The evil spirit would leave, and Saul would feel better and be all right again.'

Something to think about

Saul knew nothing about what had happened. He had no idea that Samuel had anointed David with oil in preparation for him to become the next king. David had gone back to taking care of the sheep. But God had a plan to get David trained up and ready for the future. So David ends up living in the palace taking care of King Saul, playing music for him when he gets stressed, carrying his weapons into battle and – most importantly – watching what kings do, hearing the advice they get and learning what it means to rule a country.

David is going to have to wait for God's promise to come true. He's not going to become king overnight. In the meanwhile, God has placed David in a position where he can learn and develop the skills God has given him, so that when the time comes to step up and wear the crown, he's ready.

Steve says...

I travel around the country putting on 'magic' shows with lots of tricks, illusions and escape acts, but I began by learning from a man who was already a very skilled showman, spending time with him, watching and listening and learning how to do tricks before I stepped out on my own.

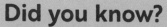

Did you know?

Even Jesus had apprentices. He chose 12 men to travel around with Him for three years, watching and listening to everything He did and said, so that when the time came, they would be able to travel the world telling people about God.

Something to talk about

· What's something really important that you've learned from someone?
· Where or how did you learn it?

Pray

Father God, help me to be a good learner. Please give me someone I can look up to and learn from as I follow You. Amen.

A mighty enemy

1 Samuel 17:3–8,10–11

'The Philistines lined up on one hill and the Israelites on another, with a valley between them. A man named Goliath, from the city of Gath, came out from the Philistine camp to challenge the Israelites. He was nearly three metres tall and wore bronze armour that weighed about 57 kilogrammes and a bronze helmet. His legs were also protected by bronze armour, and he carried a bronze javelin slung over his shoulder. His spear was as thick as the bar on a weaver's loom, and its iron head weighed about seven kilogrammes. A soldier walked in front of him carrying his shield. Goliath stood and shouted at the Israelites, "What are you doing there, lined up for battle? I am a Philistine, you slaves of Saul! Here and now I challenge the Israelite army. I dare you to pick someone to fight me!" When Saul and his men heard this, they were terrified.'

Something to think about

All was not well in Israel. Not only did they have a king who wasn't following God, they had a mighty enemy trying to attack them, and their mighty enemy had a mighty warrior: Goliath. Goliath was huge. His armour weighed more than you do. He was massive and he was strong and he terrified the Israelite soldiers. What made it even worse was that he had challenged the Israelite soldiers to a duel.

This wasn't going to be an ordinary battle between two armies. The whole future of the two countries was going to rest on a fight between two people: Goliath and whoever was brave enough to fight him. But not one Israelite soldier was.

Bekah says...

Sometimes our problems seem impossible. Whether it's a complicated maths question, needing to say sorry when we've done something wrong or starting a new project, we can feel like the Israelite army – terrified. But they'd forgotten one thing: they were God's army and God is bigger than anything we face, even Goliath.

Did you know?

Goliath beetles are the biggest beetles on the planet. They can lift a load that is 850 times heavier than their own weight!

Something to talk about

· When have you faced what seemed like an impossible task?
· How did you manage?

Pray

Father God, thank You that no problem is ever bigger than You. Help me to remember that You are on my side and nothing is impossible for You. Amen.

Know your strengths

1 Samuel 17:32–37

'David said to Saul, "Your Majesty, no one should be afraid of this Philistine! I will go and fight him."

"No," answered Saul. "How could you fight him? You're just a boy, and he has been a soldier all his life!"

"Your Majesty," David said, "I take care of my father's sheep. Whenever a lion or a bear carries off a lamb, I go after it, attack it, and rescue the lamb. And if the lion or bear turns on me, I grab it by the throat and beat it to death. I have killed lions and bears, and I will do the same to this heathen Philistine, who has defied the army of the living God. The LORD has saved me from lions and bears; he will save me from this Philistine."'

Something to think about

Later on in the Bible, we are told that David was a man after God's heart. This means he was a man who loved God and always wanted to please Him. And it means that when a giant came to frighten God's people, David understood that Goliath wasn't bigger than God. David knew that with God's help he could fight a giant, he knew that God had already put him in situations where he had learned the skills to fight bears and lions, so a giant man was no more frightening.

It seems crazy that a king would let a boy be the person to take on Goliath, but maybe he could see that this boy had the right skills, the right attitude and that God was with him.

Steve says...

I'm not very good at using computers or phones or anything to do with gadgets, but my girls are brilliant. When I get stuck, I've learned to let them fix things – they do it much better than me.

Did you know?

The Goliath bird-eater spider is one of the biggest spiders in the world – its leg span can be over 12 inches!

Something to talk about

· What skills do you have?
· How could you use these skills for God?

Pray

Father God, thank You for the many different gifts You have given me. Help me to use them for You. Amen.

Something for the weekend

Is there a new skill you'd like to learn? Why not start this weekend? (If it's a big thing, use the weekend to research and make a plan for learning your new skill.)

A big head and a small head

1 Samuel 17:48–51;57–58

'Goliath started walking towards David again, and David ran quickly toward the Philistine battle line to fight him. He put his hand into his bag and took out a stone, which he slung at Goliath. It hit him on the forehead and broke his skull, and Goliath fell face downward on the ground. And so, without a sword, David defeated and killed Goliath with a sling and a stone! He ran to him, stood over him, took Goliath's sword out of its sheath, and cut off his head and killed him. So when David returned to camp after killing Goliath, Abner took him to Saul. David was still carrying Goliath's head. Saul asked him, "Young man, whose son are you?"

"I am the son of your servant Jesse from Bethlehem," David answered.'

Something to think about

David was a hero. No two ways about it. He knew God was with him. All his life he'd been practising using his sling as he looked after the sheep, and when it mattered he stepped up to fight the enemy that no one else would. He flung a stone at the giant and cut off his great big head.

Goliath wouldn't bother God's people ever again. It would have been easy for David to get big-headed after all he'd done. He could have shown off about his bravery and skill, he could even have started talking about the fact that God had told him he would be king someday. But when he is taken to King Saul, and is asked about his family, he just answers that his dad is the king's servant – they're not a special family, just one that serves their king. It's pretty humble stuff.

Steve says...

Our girls all have different skills – some are great at dancing, some are great at maths and others can rock-climb or are brilliant at looking after children. We love to celebrate what they can do and the ways they are special, but it's also important for them to know that they're all our children and no one is more special than anyone else.

Something to talk about

· When have you done something special?
· Who did you tell about it?

Pray

Father God, thank You for making me special and unique and amazing. Help me always to remember that You made everyone that way, and that everyone is special to You. Amen.

WEEK 7:
SMALL FEET,
BIG FEATS

TUESDAY

Best friends

1 Samuel 18:1–4

'*Saul and David finished their conversation. After that, Saul's son Jonathan was deeply attracted to David and came to love him as much as he loved himself. Saul kept David with him from that day on and did not let him go back home. Jonathan swore eternal friendship with David because of his deep affection for him. He took off the robe he was wearing and gave it to David, together with his armour and also his sword, bow, and belt.*'

Something to think about

After the battle, David went to live in the king's palace where he became great friends with the prince, Jonathan. It was an unlikely friendship – normally the prince would be the next king, and yet God had promised David that it wouldn't be Jonathan, it would be him. But this friendship was special: Jonathan cared more for David and for God than he did for his future career. He put David first, shared everything he had with him, and we'll see later that he went out of his way to protect him, even though David would one day take his place on the throne. Friendship really matters to God. He created people to be in friendship with Him and with each other. It means we should work at being great friends to people, just like Jonathan and David were.

Bekah says...

Sometimes it's hard to make friends and it can feel like we're not very popular. I've struggled sometimes - at school and even as a grown-up, but one of the things I've learned is that you can always be a good friend. It's good to look for ways to be kind and friendly - and friendships nearly always follow.

Did you know?

In December 2004, a frightened young hippo – separated from his family by a devastating tsunami – made friends with a 130–year-old tortoise named Mzee. They became inseparable.

Steve says...

It's fun (and sometimes challenging!) having friends who are different from me. I was fascinated to read that chimpanzees, baboons, horses, hyenas, elephants, bats and dolphins (and apparently hippos and tortoises) are some of the animals that can form friendships for life with other creatures that aren't from their species.

Something to talk about

· Who is your best friend?
· What would you do for them?

Pray

Father God, thank You for being my very best friend.
Help me to love other people the way You love me.
Help me to be the best kind of friend to people. Amen.

Jealousy

1 Samuel 18:6–9

'As David was returning after killing Goliath and as the soldiers were coming back home, women from every town in Israel came out to meet King Saul. They were singing joyful songs, dancing, and playing tambourines and lyres. In their celebration the women sang, "Saul has killed thousands, but David tens of thousands." Saul did not like this, and he became very angry. He said, "For David they claim tens of thousands, but only thousands for me. They will be making him king next!" And so he was jealous and suspicious of David from that day on.'

Something to think about

Saul doesn't know about the secret ceremony held by Samuel to anoint David all that time ago, but he's beginning to see how popular David is and that people wish he was king. It probably frightened Saul a bit – he must have realised that he wasn't being a good king. No one was singing songs like this about him. Saul could have chosen to sort himself out, say sorry to God and choose to be a better king. Instead, he chose to be angry that someone else was getting all the attention and chose to be jealous of a boy who had only ever been loyal to him.

Bekah says...

In any situation, we always have a choice in how we respond. Sometimes it's easy to say 'I couldn't help it'. But we almost always can. We can choose to be kind or cruel, to be angry or understanding, or to be thankful for what we have or jealous of what we don't.

Steve says...

When I was ten years old, I found a plastic bag in a red phone box with over £200 in it. I was saving for a new bike at the time, but knew the money wasn't mine so my parents took it to the police station for me. A few weeks later I received a letter from the man it belonged to, saying thanks and with a crisp £1 note for my honesty.

Something to talk about

· When have you had to make a big decision about how to respond?
· What did you choose?

Pray

Father God, thank You for always giving me a choice about how I behave. Help me to choose the best way, even when it's hard. Amen.

Stand up!

1 Samuel 19:1–5

'Saul told his son Jonathan and all his officials that he planned to kill David. But Jonathan was very fond of David, and so he said to him, "My father is trying to kill you. Please be careful tomorrow morning; hide in some secret place and stay there. I will go and stand by my father in the field where you are hiding, and I will speak to him about you. If I find out anything, I will let you know."

Jonathan praised David to Saul and said, "Sir, don't do wrong to your servant David. He has never done you any wrong; on the contrary, everything he has done has been a great help to you. He risked his life when he killed Goliath, and the LORD won a great victory for Israel. When you saw it, you were glad. Why, then, do you now want to do wrong to an innocent man..."'

Something to think about

Saul's jealousy got so out of control that he wanted to kill David. That is seriously bad jealousy. He told everyone his murderous plans, including his son Jonathan. So Jonathan faced a difficult choice: play it safe and just listen to his dad's rage, or stand up for his friend, even though his dad might get angry with him too?

Jonathan chooses well: he warns David and reminds his dad of David's goodness and loyalty. That was really brave, and it was right. When we see something that we know is wrong, we face a decision too – do we speak up, or sit back and let it happen?

Bekah says...

You're unlikely to need to save someone's life, but at school or work we often hear people talking unkindly about other people. It's easy to join in or to just keep quiet and not get involved, but the best decision is to stand up for the people being talked about.

Did you know?

William Wilberforce lived over 200 years ago, at a time when slavery was normal. He stood up to tell the government that they should stop slavery, even though some people got angry with him. He changed the world for thousands of people.

Something to talk about

· When have you stood up to people doing something wrong?
· What happened?

Pray

Father God, thank You for always sticking up for us, for being for us and never against us. Help us to be like You and to stand up to unkindness wherever we see it. Amen.

Escape

1 Samuel 19:8–12

*'War with the Philistines broke out again. David attacked
them and defeated them so thoroughly that they fled. One
day an evil spirit from the Lord took control of Saul. He was
sitting in his house with his spear in his hand, and David
was there, playing his harp. Saul tried to pin David to the
wall with his spear, but David dodged, and the spear stuck
in the wall. David ran away and escaped.'*

Something to think about

David had done all the right things. He had stayed loyal
to his king, but the time had come to leave his post and
run away. David had done everything he could to build a
good friendship with the king: he had patiently endured
the king's anger, risked death in battle for the king, and had
never bragged about his successes. But Saul's bad temper
and bullying had finally gone too far, and now David had to
flee and find safety.

The Bible tells us that love is patient and kind (1 Cor. 13:4).
Sticking by our friends is really important, even when
they've upset us or are having a bad day. But there are
occasions where we need to remove ourselves from

the relationship. We can only choose our own behaviour; we can't make our friends be nice. If someone continues to be very unkind, it's OK to step away from a friendship – not to be unkind to them, but simply to protect ourselves.

Bekah says...

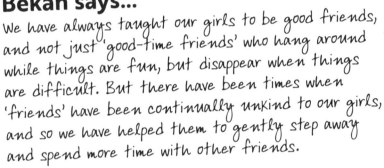

We have always taught our girls to be good friends, and not just 'good-time friends' who hang around while things are fun, but disappear when things are difficult. But there have been times when 'friends' have been continually unkind to our girls, and so we have helped them to gently step away and spend more time with other friends.

Something to talk about

- Have you ever had a friendship that you needed to walk away from?
- How did you do that?

Pray

Father God, thank You for loving me no matter what I do. Thank You for giving me examples of great friendship like Jonathan and David. Help me to be a friend who is loyal and good, but help me also to know when it's OK to step away and keep safe, like David did. Amen.

Loyal

1 Samuel 24:3–6

'[Saul] came to a cave close to some sheep pens by the road and went in to relieve himself. It happened to be the very cave in which David and his men were hiding far back in the cave. They said to him, "This is your chance! The LORD has told you that he would put your enemy in your power and you could do to him whatever you wanted to." David crept over and cut off a piece of Saul's robe without Saul's knowing it. But then David's conscience began to trouble him, and he said to his men, "May the LORD keep me from doing any harm to my master, whom the LORD chose as king! I must not harm him in the least, because he is the king chosen by the LORD!"'

Something to think about

God's promise that David would be king must have seemed like a joke. When David was winning battles, defeating giants, marrying princesses and carrying the armour of the king, God's plan seemed to make sense. But running into the night, away from the palace, away from his wife and everything he had known?

By this point in the story, David had been on the run for years. It must have seemed like everything had gone wrong. When David found Saul in the cave, he could easily have taken things into his own hands and got the plan 'back on track': but David knew that while it was necessary to step away from the king, it was wrong to kill him. David trusted God to have a plan, even though he didn't know all the details.

Something to talk about

· Have you ever found it hard to see what God is doing in your life?
· What helps you to trust God anyway?

Pray

Father God, thank You for always having a plan, even when I can't see it or understand it. Help me to trust You – no matter what. Amen.

Something for the weekend

David was an adventurer. Why not go out and do something adventurous this weekend, like go on a big bike ride, or go for a long walk and explore somewhere you've not been before?

Wow!

Psalm 8:1–2

'O LORD, our Lord,
your greatness is seen in all the world!
Your praise reaches up to the heavens;
it is sung by children and babies.
You are safe and secure from all your enemies;
you stop anyone who opposes you.
      When I look at the sky, which you have made,
at the moon and the stars, which you set in their places—
what are human beings, that you think of them;
mere mortals, that you care for them?'

Something to think about

When you stop and think about it, it's amazing that we can
talk to God. He's the King of Kings, the Lord of Lords and
the creator of the universe and yet, we get to speak to Him.
Whenever we want. Wherever we want. About anything.
It's astounding! Sometimes it's hard to know what to say to
such an awesome God, so this week let's look at how David
talks to God in Psalms 8 and 13.

Psalm 8 is a good place to start. It begins the way we
should always start talking to God: by speaking out just
how incredible God is. Sometimes we can get so carried
away with the questions we have for God that we forget
who we're talking to. It's good to remind ourselves
sometimes through the words of the psalmists.

Did you know?

The book of Psalms is a collection of ancient poetry written by lots of different followers of God. There are 150 different songs, prayers and poems.

Something to talk about

· What amazes you about God?
· How often do you tell Him? (Think about how great it feels when someone praises you, or tells you how much they love you. God also loves it when we praise Him and tell Him how much we love Him.)

Steve says...

Why not spend some time praising God, telling Him the things that are amazing about Him. You could start with the first verse of this psalm and then add your own words.

Pray

Lord, Your greatness is seen throughout the world! Your praise reaches to the heavens; I worship You because... Amen.

'Little me'

Psalm 8:3–9

'When I look at the sky, which you have made,
at the moon and the stars, which you set in their places—
what are human beings, that you think of them;
mere mortals, that you care for them?

Yet you made them inferior only to yourself;
you crowned them with glory and honour.

You appointed them rulers over everything you made;
you placed them over all creation: sheep and cattle, and
the wild animals too; the birds and the fish
and the creatures in the seas.

O LORD, our Lord,
your greatness is seen in all the world!'

Something to think about

David writes this psalm as he looks at the world all around him – the stars, the moon and the sky beyond – and he marvels at the awesomeness and majesty of God. And he realises how small he really is in comparison, even though he is God's appointed king.

Sometimes we feel like the most important person on earth, but the reality is, we're just one of billions of people. Like we said yesterday, it's shocking that we can even talk to God. But we can and He loves it when we do. God wants us to see our lives from His perspective, but that doesn't mean He wants us to feel worthless. When we remember how amazing God is, we need to remember that He chose to create us.

Bekah says...

God didn't just choose to make us along with the rest of creation: He made us rulers and guardians over everything else He made. That means we have a huge responsibility to take care of the world around us - the people, the animals and the environment.

Did you know?

There are estimated to be 8.5 million pet dogs in the UK and 8 million cats. That's a lot of furry friends!

Something to talk about

· How do you feel when you look at the incredible world around you?
· How do you feel knowing that God chose to make you?

Pray

Father God, thank You for wanting to make me. Thank You for choosing to make me. Help me to always know how special I am to You. Amen.

How long?

Psalm 13:1–3

'How much longer will you forget me, LORD? For ever?
How much longer will you hide yourself from me?
*   How long must I endure trouble?*
How long will sorrow fill my heart day and night?
How long will my enemies triumph over me?
*   Look at me, O LORD my God, and answer me.*
Restore my strength; don't let me die.
Don't let my enemies say, "We have defeated him."
Don't let them gloat over my downfall.
*   I rely on your constant love;*
I will be glad, because you will rescue me.
*   I will sing to you, O LORD,*
because you have been good to me.'

Something to think about

Talking to God is a privilege. You'd think you'd have to watch what you say. I bet you talk carefully to your head teacher or your boss at work, and I think we'd all be very polite to the Queen. But in this prayer, the writer is being downright rude to God. It's a bit shocking! I don't think any of us would speak to someone we respect like this.

But it's OK. King David wrote this psalm when his life felt really rubbish. He'd been on the run from people trying to kill him for years. So this is really just him being honest with God about how he's feeling in the moment. On our sad days and bad days, it's OK to tell God how terrible everything seems. It's OK to wonder if God is really there and to ask how long it's going to be before things get better. Now *that's* a real privilege.

Bekah says...

Some days it can feel like God has forgotten us, like He's not really there. But our feelings are not always very reliable. How we feel might seem real, but feeling something doesn't make it true.

Did you know?

King David had to wait 20 years after he was anointed king before it actually happened. That's a long wait.

Something to talk about

• How do you feel about moaning to God?
• Who else do you talk to when you're feeling sad or frustrated?

Pray

Father God, thank You that we really can talk to You about anything, even the things that make us sad or angry. Amen.

Turn to God

Psalm 13:1–6

'How much longer will you forget me, LORD? For ever?
How much longer will you hide yourself from me?
*   How long must I endure trouble?*
How long will sorrow fill my heart day and night?
How long will my enemies triumph over me?
*   Look at me, O LORD my God, and answer me.*
Restore my strength; don't let me die.
Don't let my enemies say, "We have defeated him."
Don't let them gloat over my downfall.
*   I rely on your constant love;*
I will be glad, because you will rescue me.
*   I will sing to you, O LORD,*
because you have been good to me.'

Something to think about

We're staying in Psalm 13 for a few days. You know, this prayer really does start with a moan, but it actually shows the writer is doing something right. You see, right at the beginning it shows he's talking to God. When our world falls apart, when we feel sad, lonely or frightened, we all turn to something. Some of us turn to other people we think can help us. Some of us try to distract ourselves with books, games or shopping. Sometimes we take our feelings out on other people.

King David knows better. He knows the best thing to do is to turn to God, even when he's angry and upset and feels like God's forgotten him. Those feelings of ours can make us do all the wrong things. When we're worried, the very best thing is to turn to God and ask Him for help, but sometimes we need to remind ourselves to do this.

Steve says...

When I don't want to think about sad things that are happening, I often watch TV to distract myself. The thing is, when the TV is turned off, the problem is still there. It's actually better to talk about what's happening, and God is the absolute best person to talk with.

Did you know?

This type of psalm or prayer is called a 'lament'.
There are more than 60 of them in the book of Psalms
– that's a lot of turning to God in hard times.

Something to talk about

· Who or what do you often turn to when you're frightened or sad?
· How could you remind yourself to turn to God?

Pray

Father God, sometimes when I'm frightened and upset, I forget that You are there. Thank You that I can always turn to You and talk with You. Please help me to remember to turn to You first. Amen.

Ask for help

Psalm 13:3–6

'Look at me, O Lord my God, and answer me.
Restore my strength; don't let me die.
Don't let my enemies say, "We have defeated him."
Don't let them gloat over my downfall.
    I rely on your constant love;
I will be glad, because you will rescue me.
    I will sing to you, O Lord,
because you have been good to me.'

Something to think about

Some of us are not very good at asking for help. Maybe we're a bit proud and don't like to admit when we can't do things. Maybe we're worried about bothering people or causing a fuss.

But David is really good at it, and after letting God know how sad and lost he feels, he asks God to help change things.

When we ask God to do things for us, we're not just asking for help, we're actually saying, 'God, I know You can do this. I know You're big and powerful and able to change the world around me.' And the wonderful thing about asking God for help is that He then takes our problems and He loves to help us.

Later in the Bible, another writer says to 'Leave all your worries with [God], because he cares for you' (1 Pet. 5:7). How wonderful!

Bekah says...

Last year, our 14-year-old daughter was home alone when a little fire started. She was very afraid but called the fire brigade who came and rescued her, and our house.

Did you know?

The UK's 999 emergency telephone number began in 1947 and now handles more than 30 million calls a year.

Something to talk about

· Who do you ask for help?
· Who do you help?

Steve says...

Is there something you need to ask God to help you with? Why not ask now?

Pray

Father God, thank You for loving us so much and for always wanting to help us. Thank You for the knowledge that *nothing* is more powerful than You. Amen.

Remember who God is

Psalm 13:1–6

'How much longer will you forget me, LORD? For ever?
How much longer will you hide yourself from me?
*   How long must I endure trouble?*
How long will sorrow fill my heart day and night?
How long will my enemies triumph over me?
*   Look at me, O LORD my God, and answer me.*
Restore my strength; don't let me die.
Don't let my enemies say, "We have defeated him."
Don't let them gloat over my downfall.
*   I rely on your constant love;*
I will be glad, because you will rescue me.
*   I will sing to you, O LORD,*
because you have been good to me.'

Something to think about

This psalm is great for helping us to pray in sad times.
It starts by turning to God, then saying how we feel and
asking for help. But what comes next is really important.
David doesn't just sit and talk about all that is wrong.
Instead, he chooses to focus in on what he knows about God.
He remembers that God is good and His love never ends, and
he remembers that God is a fantastic rescuer! And that gets
David so excited that he starts singing about it!

Prayer isn't just getting words out: it's talking with God, and when we do, it changes things in us. Telling God about our problems, asking for help and remembering everything we know about Him can change how we feel as God's Holy Spirit brings us peace and joy. Prayer is powerful!

Bekah says...

I have kept a journal since I was a teenager and sometimes I have written my prayers out to God when I'm feeling sad. It helps me to process how I'm feeling and it always amazes me how through my written prayers, God changes how I feel as I focus on Him.

Something to talk about

· What makes you feel better when you are sad?
· Who helps you feel better?

Steve says...

If there's something that's bothering you right now, why not write a prayer of lament? Remember: turn to God, tell Him how you're feeling, ask for help, focus on who God is – and then praise Him.

Pray

Father God, thank You for being more powerful than my problems. Help me to focus on Your greatness, and not on my fears. Amen.

Something for the weekend

If you go to church this weekend, really focus on singing songs of praise to God as you remember just how wonderful He is.

WEEK 9:
HIS BEAUTY IN
OUR MESS

MONDAY

Sorry

Psalm 32:1–5

'Happy are those whose sins are forgiven,
whose wrongs are pardoned.
Happy is the one whom the LORD does not accuse of
doing wrong
and who is free from all deceit.
    When I did not confess my sins,
I was worn out from crying all day long.
Day and night you punished me, LORD;
my strength was completely drained,
as moisture is dried up by the summer heat.
    Then I confessed my sins to you;
I did not conceal my wrongdoings.
I decided to confess them to you,
and you forgave all my sins.'

Something to think about

Have you ever found it hard to look someone in the eye?
Not because your eyes are tired or it's dark, but because
you've done something wrong or let someone down and
you don't know how to tell them? It's a horrible feeling.
Sometimes we can be like that with God. We've done
something wrong and we don't know how to face Him, so
we avoid Him. King David was a great king, but he did some
really bad things – he even had a man killed! And yet, the
Bible describes him as a man after God's own heart.

Psalm 32 gives us an idea of how we should pray when we've let God down, how we can mess up and still be someone who has a close relationship with God. It starts like every prayer: by choosing to talk to God, even when it feels hard.

Steve says...

Once when I was travelling, I was staying in the home of someone I'd never met before. They had been kind enough to give me a place to stay, but when I went to my bedroom I broke the blinds and then had to go back downstairs to tell them. That was a conversation I didn't want to have, but it would have been worse not to tell them!

Did you know?
King David had a man called Uriah killed because David wanted to marry Uriah's wife! No wonder he felt bad!

Something to talk about
· Have you ever really let someone down?
· How did you deal with it?

Pray
Father God, thank You for all the examples in the Bible of people who let You down but who were able to still talk to You about their lives. Thank You that there is nothing I can do to stop You talking with me. Amen.

Cover up

Psalm 32:1–5

'Happy are those whose sins are forgiven,
whose wrongs are pardoned.
Happy is the one whom the LORD does not accuse of doing
wrong
and who is free from all deceit.
When I did not confess my sins,
I was worn out from crying all day long.
Day and night you punished me, LORD;
my strength was completely drained,
as moisture is dried up by the summer heat.
Then I confessed my sins to you;
I did not conceal my wrongdoings.
I decided to confess them to you,
and you forgave all my sins.'

Something to think about

We read a story in the news once about a lady who had
gone to the loo on a first date and then couldn't flush it
properly. That's always embarrassing, but what the lady
did next was crazy! She didn't want her new boyfriend to
see her poo, so she picked it out of the toilet and tried to
throw it out of the window. But she didn't realise there was
a second pane of glass and so her poo got stuck between
the two windows. It got worse – she then got stuck trying
to remove it from between the windows and in the end the
fire brigade had to come and rescue her!

What a lot of fuss to try to hide a poo. But we often try to hide our mess so that people don't find out about some of the things we've done. But hiding the truth leaves us feeling like David – guilty, frightened and unhappy. It's always better to own up to what we've done and be honest, and it's always good to tell God.

Bekah says...

When I was a teenager, I had a party when my parents were away that got out of hand. I did everything I could to clear up afterwards to hide the evidence, but I felt much better when I just admitted what had happened.

Something to talk about

· What's the hardest thing you've had to own up to?
· How did you deal with it?

Pray

God, thank You that we can always tell You what we've done, no matter how ashamed we feel. Thank You for always forgiving us, and helping us to change. Amen.

WEEK 9:
HIS BEAUTY IN OUR MESS

WEDNESDAY

Confession time

Psalm 32:5–7

'Then I confessed my sins to you;
I did not conceal my wrongdoings.
I decided to confess them to you,
and you forgave all my sins.
  So all your loyal people should pray to you in times of need;
when a great flood of trouble comes rushing in,
it will not reach them.
You are my hiding place;
you will save me from trouble.
I sing aloud of your salvation,
because you protect me.'

Something to think about

'I confessed my sins to you' is a sentence with a lot of strange words. 'Confessed' means admitted, and 'sins' are the things we do wrong. David didn't try to hide his wrongdoings. He owned up to them, told God and then something amazing happened... God forgave him. Forgiving doesn't mean that the wrong never happened, or didn't matter, or even that there won't be any consequences – but it means that when God looks at us He doesn't see our sin anymore: He doesn't stay angry. He sees us as pure and holy and we don't need to feel bad anymore. In fact, it makes David feel so much better that he says everyone should tell God when they've done something wrong, and let Him protect them.

Bekah says...

Do you know what? You can only give away what you own. That's true with physical things, but it's also true with the things we do. When we 'own' up to the bad things we've done, we can give them away to God.

Did you know?

God loves to forgive us. It's why He allowed Jesus to be killed on the cross, so that Jesus would take all the punishment for our sins. It means we can always know we're safe, telling Him what we've done. Jesus has already dealt with it and is waiting to forgive us, and to help us fix things that we couldn't have fixed on our own.

Something to talk about

• Why is it hard to admit when we've done something wrong?
• How can you make it easier for those in your family to tell you if they've made mistakes?

Steve says...

Is there is something on your mind that you know you need to confess to someone? Why not talk to God about it now, ask Him to help you, and then go and tell the other person.

Pray

Father God, thank You for always being ready to forgive me. Help me to own up to my mistakes and give them to You to forgive. Amen.

When no one understands

Psalm 139:1–6

'LORD, you have examined me and you know me.
You know everything I do;
from far away you understand all my thoughts.
You see me, whether I am working or resting;
you know all my actions.
Even before I speak,
you already know what I will say.
You are all round me on every side;
you protect me with your power.
Your knowledge of me is too deep;
it is beyond my understanding.'

Something to think about

Can you imagine if all your thoughts were constantly playing out loud through a speaker, like a radio show? That could be awkward! There are some thoughts I'd rather other people didn't know I was having. But in this prayer, David knows that God is aware of everything that he thinks and does.

But this doesn't make David feel awkward, it makes him feel safe. It makes him feel safe because he knows God always understands how he feels and what he means. It means that on the days when it feels like no one understands you, God always will. Again, David is praying what he knows to be true about God, reassuring himself that God always understands.

Bekah says...

We have teenage daughters and they often feel like no one understands them - not at school, not at home, not even their friends. This is one of their favourite psalms to read because it reminds them that God is always with them and that He gets them.

Did you know?

According to the Linguistic Society, there are 6,909 living languages in the world. God understands everyone, no matter what language they speak.

Something to talk about

· Who do you find easy to talk to?
· Is there something you wish people understood about you?

Steve says...

I once got in a real pickle being misunderstood in France. My French isn't very good and when a policeman asked me what I was doing, I thought I explained that I was an escapologist... but I actually said I was a Peeping Tom. Oops.

Pray

Father God, it's amazing that You know every thought in my head. It's hard to even take that in. Thank You for knowing me, for loving me and for protecting me. Amen.

Perfectly put together

Psalm 139:13–16

'You created every part of me;
you put me together in my mother's womb.
I praise you because you are to be feared;
all you do is strange and wonderful.
I know it with all my heart.
When my bones were being formed,
carefully put together in my mother's womb,
when I was growing there in secret,
you knew that I was there —
you saw me before I was born.'

Something to think about

These are some of my favourite verses in the Bible. There are days when I wish I looked different, when I wish I was smarter, and when I feel like maybe no one would care if I wasn't here. But this prayer of David's reminds me that that's just not true. If I pray this prayer with David, I remember that nobody is a mistake; God put me together in my mum's tummy. He planned me, He carefully made me, He chose to make me – just the way I am.

And it's the same for you. God made you. He loves you just the way you are: you are *wonderfully* made. We live in a world that constantly tells us who we should look like, walk like and talk like. We live in a world that tells us which gadgets we should own to be cool, which games we should play to be in the 'in crowd' and which TV programmes we should watch to be acceptable. But God doesn't give a monkey's about any of that. He looks at you as He has looked at you since before you were born... and He thinks you're marvellous.

Did you know?

In 2015, the BBC reported that there were 51,140 people in the UK who chose to have cosmetic surgery to change the way they look.

Something to talk about

• Is there anything you wish you could change about yourself?
• How does it feel to know that God thinks you're brilliant?

Pray

Father God, sometimes I don't feel brilliant. In fact, there are days when I feel worthless. So it's wonderful when I remember that You chose to make me just the way I am, and that I am wonderful to You. Please help me to see myself the way You do. Amen.

Change me

Psalm 139:23–24

'Examine me, O God, and know my mind;
test me, and discover my thoughts.
Find out if there is any evil in me
and guide me in the everlasting way.'

Something to think about

This week we've looked at how to pray when we feel bad about the things we've done, how to pray when we remember that God is more awesome than we can understand, and how to pray when we feel small and useless. But today's part of the prayer is a lot more challenging.

David invites God to look at every thought in his head and point out what isn't good. That's brave. But David asks this because, more than anything, he wanted to be close to God and to become more like Him; so he's asking God to help him become a better person. It's like being a parent. I love my children no matter what they do, but I want to help them learn new things, develop self-control and to be kind and loving so they can enjoy great friendships. Loving people doesn't mean pretending they never do anything wrong: it means helping them to become the best they can be.

Bekah says...

When I was a teenager, I asked God the same question as David, and over the next few days I became really aware of my nasty temper and how unkind I sometimes was to my brother. It was God letting me know that this was something He'd like me to change, so I asked Him to help me be more patient and kind. Then I tried very hard to be nicer to my brother.

Something to talk about

· When have you known that God wanted you to change your behaviour?
· How did you know?

Steve says...

It's easy to ask God to fix things for us, or to give us nice things, but to show us how to be a better person? That needs us to be really humble, really believing that God knows best and trusting Him to show us the best way. Do you dare to do it?

Pray

Dear God, thank You so much for loving me no matter what I do, but also for loving me enough to want me to become the best I can be. Please keep working on the inside of me. Amen.

Something for the weekend

Why not go and find a nice notebook that you can use as a family prayer diary? You could decorate it together and then use it each day to write your prayers and the answers God gives you.

Willing

Luke 1:30–38

'The angel said to her, "Don't be afraid, Mary; God has been gracious to you. You will become pregnant and give birth to a son, and you will name him Jesus. He will be great and will be called the Son of the Most High God. The Lord God will make him a king, as his ancestor David was, and he will be the king of the descendants of Jacob forever; his kingdom will never end!"

Mary said to the angel, "I am a virgin. How, then, can this be?"

The angel answered, "The Holy Spirit will come on you, and God's power will rest upon you. For this reason the holy child will be called the Son of God. Remember your relative Elizabeth. It is said that she cannot have children, but she herself is now six months pregnant, even though she is very old. For there is nothing that God cannot do."

"I am the Lord's servant," said Mary; "may it happen to me as you have said." And the angel left her.'

Something to think about

This is the beginning of the best-known story in the world! The story of when God sent His Son, Jesus, to come and live as a man. Jesus spent more than 30 years on earth, meeting all kinds of people along the way. But Mary was the first, as she carried Jesus in her tummy for nine months.

It was a huge honour to be chosen to be Jesus' mum, but it was risky too. Mary wasn't married yet, so she could get into lots of trouble. But when the angel comes to tell her, she doesn't hesitate or worry, she just says, 'I'm here to serve God'. Wow, what an amazing servant to God she was.

Did you know?

Charles Wesley's *Hark! The Herald Angels Sing* is one of the most popular carols that we sing each Christmas. But did you know that it sounds completely different today than when it was written in 1739 as the words and tune have been changed?

Something to talk about

· What does being a servant mean?
· How do you feel about being a servant?

Pray

Father God, You are wonderful, and the fact that You choose to use us to be part of Your plan is amazing. Help me to say 'yes' like Mary, and be Your willing servant always. Amen.

Favoured

Luke 1:39–44

'Soon afterwards Mary got ready and hurried off to a town in the hill country of Judea. She went into Zechariah's house and greeted Elizabeth. When Elizabeth heard Mary's greeting, the baby moved within her. Elizabeth was filled with the Holy Spirit and said in a loud voice, "You are the most blessed of all women, and blessed is the child you will bear! Why should this great thing happen to me, that my Lord's mother comes to visit me? For as soon as I heard your greeting, the baby within me jumped with gladness."'

Something to think about

Elizabeth was Mary's cousin, and she was having a miracle baby of her own. When she meets pregnant Mary, her baby jumps and dances within her and Elizabeth knows that she is in the presence of something or somebody special. Jesus wasn't even born yet, but Elizabeth already recognised Him as Lord. It's hard to imagine how that could be, but it's amazing and she knows she is blessed to have even met His mum.

So often people didn't recognise Jesus, or just saw Him as an ordinary man, or a good teacher. They missed that He was special, that He was God. It's the same today. We can read stories about Jesus and maybe even talk to Him, but it's good to stop and remind ourselves that He is no ordinary man – He's the Son of God.

Steve says...

I once bumped into my mate Rob at the airport and started to chat to him. He looked confused and then I realised he wasn't my mate at all, I just recognised him because he was the singer Robin Gibb from the band the Bee Gees!

Did you know?

Prosopagnosia is the name for 'face blindness'. People with prosopagnosia can't recognise people by their face – not even their family. They have to know them by the way they walk, talk or even their clothing!

Something to talk about

· When did you first recognise just who Jesus was?
· How did that make you feel?

Pray

Father God, help me to know You completely, to see through the stories I know so well and to meet the Son of God properly. Amen.

Praising

Luke 2:8–11,16–20

'There were some shepherds in that part of the country who were spending the night in the fields, taking care of their flocks. An angel of the Lord appeared to them, and the glory of the Lord shone over them. They were terribly afraid, but the angel said to them, "Don't be afraid! I am here with good news for you, which will bring great joy to all the people. This very day in David's town your Saviour was born — Christ the Lord!

So they hurried off and found Mary and Joseph and saw the baby lying in the manger. When the shepherds saw him, they told them what the angel had said about the child. All who heard it were amazed at what the shepherds said. Mary remembered all these things and thought deeply about them. The shepherds went back, singing praises to God for all they had heard and seen; it had been just as the angel had told them.'

Something to think about

Shepherds were the down-and-outs of the day, the rough-and-tumble nobodies. Yet they were among the first people invited (by God, no less) to meet the baby Jesus. It must have been the most amazingly crazy time. First, they saw angels singing in the sky, then they found the baby just as they had been told and, like Elizabeth, they realised He was no ordinary baby.

It would have been mind-blowing and it changed something about these rough, tough shepherds. Singing songs to God and talking about babies was not what they normally did, but this baby had changed all that. They met Jesus – and just couldn't stop talking about Him and praising God for sending His Son to earth.

Steve says...

I love telling people about Jesus. Like the shepherds, I know that Jesus is the best news I've ever heard, and good news is for sharing! I've spent my life travelling around the country, telling people about Jesus.

Something to talk about
· What's the best news you've ever heard?
· Who did you tell?

Bekah says...

Jesus was great news for the shepherds and He is still the ultimate good news for us today. Is there someone you could share that news with?

Pray
Father God, thank You for sending Your Son from heaven to earth to save us. It's the most amazing news – help me to tell someone about it today. Amen.

Giving

Matthew 2:1–2,10–11

'Jesus was born in the town of Bethlehem in Judea, during the time when Herod was king. Soon afterwards, some men who studied the stars came from the east to Jerusalem and asked, "Where is the baby born to be the king of the Jews? We saw his star when it came up in the east, and we have come to worship him."

When they saw it, how happy they were, what joy was theirs! It went ahead of them until it stopped over the place where the child was. They went into the house, and when they saw the child with his mother Mary, they knelt down and worshipped him. They brought out their gifts of gold, frankincense, and myrrh, and presented them to him.'

Something to think about

The wise men travelled hundreds of miles to find the King they'd studied and read about. They left their homes and followed a star for weeks to meet Jesus. They knew before they even met Him that He was the King of God's people, the Jews. They knew He was special, they knew He was worth the time and cost of their hard journey and they knew He was worth their worship and their gifts.

When the wise men arrived and finally met Jesus, they didn't try to impress Him or teach Him their wisdom, they didn't ask Him for anything. Instead, they gave Him their most valuable things – gold, frankincense and myrrh, and they knelt to give Him their worship. They held nothing back.

Bekah says...

The wise men were important people and they had great things, but when they met Jesus they realised He was more important than anything else. It's really easy to make other things in our day-to-day life more important than Jesus, but Jesus is bigger and better and deserves to come first in our life.

Did you know?

The wise men who came to see the baby Jesus only appear in Matthew's Christmas story, but he never mentioned their names. Gaspar, Melchior and Balthasar were all added by storytellers over the centuries. And there might have been hundreds of wise men, not just three, galloping on their camels to worship the little boy.

Something to talk about

· What's the most valuable thing you've ever had?
· What could make you give it up?

Pray

Father God, You gave me everything I have. Thank You. Help me not to make my things and my 'wants' more important than You. Amen.

Threatened

Matthew 2:13–16

'After they had left, an angel of the Lord appeared in a dream to Joseph and said, "Herod will be looking for the child in order to kill him. So get up, take the child and his mother and escape to Egypt, and stay there until I tell you to leave."

Joseph got up, took the child and his mother, and left during the night for Egypt, where he stayed until Herod died. This was done to make what the Lord had said through the prophet come true, "I called my Son out of Egypt."

When Herod realized that the visitors from the east had tricked him, he was furious. He gave orders to kill all the boys in Bethlehem and its neighbourhood who were two years old and younger — this was done in accordance with what he had learned from the visitors about the time when the star had appeared.'

Something to think about

It's easy to think that anyone who met Jesus would just love Him. Mary, Elizabeth, the shepherds and the wise men all did. But not Herod. Herod just felt threatened by Him and tried to get rid of Jesus. Herod had heard that this baby might be the new king and he was worried he'd lose his throne. He was worried that Jesus would change his world... and he liked it just as it was.

We can be the same. Jesus looks great, but actually getting to know Him could change our lives in ways we may feel we're not ready for. He might want us to give up some things we like doing, or to do things that frighten us. So we try to avoid Him and pretend He's not there.

Steve says...

Knowing Jesus has totally changed my life. When I left school I worked in a bank and I was very happy. But God told me to change everything and spend all my days telling people about Jesus. It was scary starting something new. But it was worth it!

Something to talk about

· How has knowing Jesus changed your life?
· Has that been hard or easy, or somewhere in between?

Pray

Jesus, thank You for loving me and being my best friend, even before I knew You were there. Help me to trust You and follow You even when that changes my world. And thank You that even when something is scary or hard, You always lead me to something that is even better! Amen.

Ready

Luke 2:25–32

'At that time there was a man named Simeon living in Jerusalem. He was a good, God-fearing man and was waiting for Israel to be saved. The Holy Spirit was with him and had assured him that he would not die before he had seen the Lord's promised Messiah. Led by the Spirit, Simeon went into the Temple. When the parents brought the child Jesus into the Temple to do for him what the Law required, Simeon took the child in his arms and gave thanks to God:

"Now, Lord, you have kept your promise,
and you may let your servant go in peace.
With my own eyes I have seen your salvation,
which you have prepared in the presence of all peoples:
A light to reveal your will to the Gentiles
and bring glory to your people Israel."'

Something to think about

This is an unusual story – the kind most people won't experience for themselves, but Simeon was a man who had a promise from God that he would live to see the Saviour of the world. Imagine that!

But like so many other people in the Bible, he had been waiting a very long time. He was an old man when Mary and Joseph brought Jesus to the temple, but when Simeon saw Him, he knew that this young boy was the Saviour he had been waiting for. He held Jesus in his arms, thanking God. Meeting Jesus was all he had ever wanted, and he recognised Him immediately and knew that this meeting was enough: now he was ready to go and be with God.

Something to talk about
· What have you waited a long time for?
· How did it feel when it finally arrived?

Pray
Lord Jesus, thank You that You are enough: You were all that Simeon had been waiting for, and You are all I need too. Help me to remember that, on the days when I get distracted or put my hopes in other things instead of You. Please help me keep my focus on You. Amen.

Something for the weekend
Every December, we celebrate Christmas – God sending His Son to us. But the truth is, it's worth celebrating all year round. Have you got a family Christmas tradition you could do this weekend, even if it's the middle of summer?

Beaten!

Luke 4:1–8

'Jesus returned from the Jordan full of the Holy Spirit and was led by the Spirit into the desert, where he was tempted by the Devil for forty days. In all that time he ate nothing, so that he was hungry when it was over. The Devil said to him, "If you are God's Son, order this stone to turn into bread." But Jesus answered, "The scripture says, 'Human beings cannot live on bread alone.'" Then the Devil took him up and showed him in a second all the kingdoms of the world. "I will give you all this power and all this wealth," the Devil told him. "It has all been handed over to me, and I can give it to anyone I choose. All this will be yours, then, if you worship me." Jesus answered, "The scripture says, 'Worship the Lord your God and serve only him!'"'

Something to think about

Not everyone who met Jesus was excited about it or full of joy. Not everyone had been waiting all their life to meet the Saviour of the world. The devil had known God forever – but still chose to be His enemy. When he met Jesus he just wanted to destroy Him. The devil visited Jesus when He was all alone in the desert, and spent 40 days trying to make Jesus do something wrong. He knew Jesus was feeling weak and hungry and alone and thought this was his opportunity to trip Him up.

But he was disappointed. Even when feeling hungry, alone and weak, Jesus trusted God and knew what the Bible said and He stayed true to who He was.

Bekah says...

The more I read the Bible, the more I get to know God and understand how I should live my life. Every day, there are things I could easily do that wouldn't be best for me or the people around me. Knowing the Bible and knowing God helps me to choose to do the best thing and follow Him.

Something to talk about

· When have you been tempted to do something you shouldn't?
· How did you manage to stay true to God?

Steve says...

Why don't you choose a different Bible verse each week to learn as a family?

Pray

Father God, I want to stay true to You. Help me to know You better, to know Your Bible and to see through the devil's tricks and stand up to him when he tries to trip me up. Amen.

Unworthy

Luke 5:5–11

'"Master," Simon answered, "we worked hard all night long and caught nothing. But if you say so, I will let down the nets." They let them down and caught such a large number of fish that the nets were about to break. So they motioned to their partners in the other boat to come and help them. They came and filled both boats so full of fish that the boats were about to sink. When Simon Peter saw what had happened, he fell on his knees before Jesus and said, "Go away from me, Lord! I am a sinful man!" He and the others with him were all amazed at the large number of fish they had caught. The same was true of Simon's partners, James and John, the sons of Zebedee. Jesus said to Simon, "Don't be afraid; from now on you will be catching people." They pulled the boats up on the beach, left everything, and followed Jesus.'

Something to think about

This is an amazing story. Simon and the other fishermen know that Jesus is special. But when He helps them to catch a miraculous amount of fish, they realise He's more than just 'special'. And something strange happens to Simon: as he realises how wonderful Jesus is, he realises how bad he is in comparison and that he's not good enough to be near Jesus. And he's totally right.

But Jesus loves Simon and the others, and asks them to come on a journey with Him, even though they're not perfect. Every single one of them is so proud to be asked, they leave everything behind and start the journey of a lifetime with Jesus.

Bekah says...

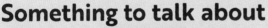

We don't always like to think about being wrong or imperfect. But the truth is: we are. But the even greater truth is that Jesus loves us anyway and wants us to go on a journey with Him. Will you follow?

Something to talk about

· When did you choose to follow Jesus?
· Did you need to leave anything behind?

Steve says...

If you've never chosen to follow Jesus, maybe it's time to do that today.

Pray

Dear Jesus, I know I can never be good enough for You on my own. Thank You for loving me anyway and inviting me to come on a journey with You. I choose to follow You. Amen.

Sure

Luke 5:12–14

'Once Jesus was in a town where there was a man who was suffering from a dreaded skin disease. When he saw Jesus, he threw himself down and begged him, "Sir, if you want to, you can make me clean!" Jesus stretched out his hand and touched him. "I do want to," he answered. "Be clean!" At once the disease left the man. Jesus ordered him, "Don't tell anyone, but go straight to the priest and let him examine you; then to prove to everyone that you are cured, offer the sacrifice as Moses ordered."'

Something to think about

We don't even know the name of this man who met Jesus; we just know that he had a pretty nasty disease that meant no one would talk to him, and he was pretty confident that Jesus had the power to change that. This man would have been ignored by everyone, but he dared to talk to Jesus: he was brave enough to ask Jesus to listen to him, to take away his disease and change his world.

So Jesus did. In fact, Jesus did more than that: He touched him. Other people would have been so scared of catching this man's disease that they wouldn't have gone anywhere near him. Bystanders would probably have moved away as he came near to Jesus. Jesus took away the disease – but more importantly, He came close to the man and became his friend. Now that's an amazing meeting.

Steve says...

For many years I used to dangle upside-down from cranes while escaping from strait-jackets, to tell large crowds how Jesus could set them free. I had to put total trust in my technical team on the ground, the crane driver and my ankle harnesses to keep me safe and sound.

Did you know?

In 1982 a cure was developed for leprosy, but there are still over 200,000 new cases of leprosy diagnosed each year. You can find out more on the Leprosy Mission website.

Something to talk about
· What are you sure you know about God?
· How does this make you behave?

Bekah says...

Why not write down some of the things you know about God and then thank Him for them.

Pray
Father God, thank You that You are good, that You are powerful and that You love me. Amen.

Restored

Luke 7:11–15

'Soon afterwards Jesus went to a town called Nain, accompanied by his disciples and a large crowd. Just as he arrived at the gate of the town, a funeral procession was coming out. The dead man was the only son of a woman who was a widow, and a large crowd from the town was with her. When the Lord saw her, his heart was filled with pity for her, and he said to her, "Don't cry." Then he walked over and touched the coffin, and the men carrying it stopped. Jesus said, "Young man! Get up, I tell you!" The dead man sat up and began to talk, and Jesus gave him back to his mother.'

Something to think about

This is another story with an unnamed person. It's about a lady who had already lost her husband, and now she's lost her son. She's lost everything. She's not looking for Jesus, she hasn't asked Him to help her. She's just trying to bury her son. Her whole world has fallen apart. But Jesus knows her, and as He walks past her, He sees her sadness. He tells her not to cry anymore and tells her dead son to get up! In the length of one sentence, that lady's world came back together in a way she could never have imagined. Without even looking for Him, she had a life-changing meeting with Jesus.

Bekah says...

God surprises us all the time, even when we're not looking. Ten years ago I was on holiday with my children, minding my own business, when I met this friendly, handsome man. I hadn't asked God to do it, but He'd just introduced me to the man who was going to be my husband. My world changed in a moment.

Did you know?

Pirates of the Caribbean star, Johnny Depp, regularly visits children's hospitals around the world dressed as his character Captain Jack Sparrow, to surprise and cheer up poorly children. He poses for photos, hands out gifts, and even has a few foam-sword duels with the more adventurous young patients.

Something to talk about

· Has God ever done something surprising in your life?
· How did that change your world?

Pray

Father God, thank You for knowing what I need better than I do. Help me to notice all the amazing things You do for me. Amen.

Learn

Luke 10:38–42

'As Jesus and his disciples went on their way, he came to a village where a woman named Martha welcomed him in her home. She had a sister named Mary, who sat down at the feet of the Lord and listened to his teaching. Martha was upset over all the work she had to do, so she came and said, "Lord, don't you care that my sister has left me to do all the work by myself? Tell her to come and help me!" The Lord answered her, "Martha, Martha! You are worried and troubled over so many things, but just one is needed. Mary has chosen the right thing, and it will not be taken away from her."'

Something to think about

Mary and Martha were sisters. When I read this story, I can almost imagine them competing and disagreeing when they were young. They're very different people. Jesus comes to visit them, and Martha runs around trying to make everything nice, while Mary just sits with Jesus and listens to all He has to say. Martha is cross with Mary for not doing anything, but Jesus stops her because He knows that Mary, in this case, is doing the right thing. Jesus doesn't care about the food or the tidy house, He wants to get to know these women. Martha is trying to impress Jesus; Mary just wants to listen and learn from Him.

Bekah says...

Sometimes we can be so busy running around trying to do the right thing, we don't stop to get to know Jesus. We think we know what He'd like us to do, but actually, more than anything He wants us to stop and get to know Him better.

Something to talk about

· How easy do you find it to sit still and spend time with Jesus?
· What have you learned about Jesus recently?

Steve says...

Here's a challenge: why not see if you can spend four minutes a day talking to Jesus? Spend one minute telling Him why He's awesome, one minute apologizing for things you're sorry for, one minute thanking Him for things you're grateful for and one minute asking for things you're hoping for. I think you might find you need more time...

Pray

Father God, it's amazing to realise that You like to spend time with us. Help us to stop and listen to You, even in the 'busy-ness' of our days. Amen.

Important

Luke 18:15–17

'Some people brought their babies to Jesus for him to place his hands on them. The disciples saw them and scolded them for doing so, but Jesus called the children to him and said, "Let the children come to me and do not stop them, because the Kingdom of God belongs to such as these. Remember this! Whoever does not receive the Kingdom of God like a child will never enter it."'

Something to think about

'Children should be seen but not heard.' That's something that used to be said by my grandparents' generation. I think it was probably the same when Jesus was alive too. The disciples got angry because people were 'bothering' Jesus with their children. But here's the thing: Jesus *loves* children. He didn't feel bothered by them: He loved the fact that children didn't try to impress Him or try to be something they weren't – they just came and enjoyed His company, a bit like Mary from yesterday's reading.

Even today, it can seem like children aren't as important: grown-ups make all the big decisions and you have to do as you're told. Often that's the way it needs to be, but it doesn't mean you're not important, and it doesn't mean you're not loved. Jesus loves you, no matter how old you are, how clever you are, how noisy you are or how good you are. Never forget that.

Bekah says...

I've always loved working with children. I used to be a teacher, and I really enjoy teaching older children. I especially like teenagers, even when they're grumpy and moody. But some of my teacher friends preferred teaching younger children – even when they can't sit still.

Did you know?

It is thought that an average of 353,000 babies are born each day around the world. That's a lot of children!

Something to talk about

· Grown-ups – what were you like as a child?
· Children – what do you think you'll be like as a grown-up?

Pray

Father God, we're all Your children, and You love every one of us. Thank You for loving me just as I am, no matter what age I am. Help me to love people like You do. Amen.

Something for the weekend

Around the world, 600 million children live in extreme poverty. Why not do something to help? You could raise money for a children's charity (like Compassion UK), or if you sponsor a child, write them a letter to remind them that you care and that Jesus cares?

Tested

Luke 18:18,22–26

'A Jewish leader asked Jesus, "Good Teacher, what must I do to receive eternal life?" When Jesus heard this, he said to him, "There is still one more thing you need to do. Sell all you have and give the money to the poor, and you will have riches in heaven; then come and follow me." But when the man heard this, he became very sad, because he was very rich. Jesus saw that he was sad and said, "How hard it is for rich people to enter the Kingdom of God! It is much harder for a rich person to enter the Kingdom of God than for a camel to go through the eye of a needle." The people who heard him asked, "Who, then, can be saved?"'

Something to think about

The young man in this story is a good man. He's a synagogue leader who has spent his life trying to follow God's laws. He really wants to go to heaven and he's come to meet Jesus, hoping that Jesus will help him with this. But Jesus doesn't help in the way he'd like. In fact, this 'test' is similar to the test God set for Abraham when He asked him to sacrifice Isaac. Jesus can see that this man tries hard to keep the rules, but He can also see what this man loves the most – his money. So Jesus asks him to give his money up for God. It's the one thing the man won't do. He loves his money more than he loves God.

Bekah says...

The love of money is one of the things that the Bible often talks about being a problem for people. Everyone needs money to buy food and have a home, but when we start being obsessed with having more and more and not wanting to share it with people? Then there's a real problem.

Did you know?

The eight richest people on earth have the same amount of money between them as the poorest half of the world – that's roughly 3.6 billion people. Imagine if they shared their money out – what a difference that could make!

Something to talk about

· Who would you choose to give some of your money to?
· Why would you do that?

Pray

Father God, thank You that I get to sleep in a bed at night and have food on my table. Help me always to be ready to share what I have with other people. Amen.

Surprised

Luke 19:1–6

'Jesus went on into Jericho and was passing through. There was a chief tax collector there named Zacchaeus, who was rich. He was trying to see who Jesus was, but he was a little man and could not see Jesus because of the crowd. So he ran ahead of the crowd and climbed a sycamore tree to see Jesus, who was going to pass that way. When Jesus came to that place, he looked up and said to Zacchaeus, "Hurry down, Zacchaeus, because I must stay in your house today." Zacchaeus hurried down and welcomed him with great joy. All the people who saw it started grumbling, "This man has gone as a guest to the home of a sinner!" Zacchaeus stood up and said to the Lord, "Listen, sir! I will give half my belongings to the poor, and if I have cheated anyone, I will pay back four times as much."'

Something to think about

Zacchaeus is the opposite of the man we met yesterday. He was not a good man. He had been taking other people's money and working for the enemy, the Romans, for years. When he meets Jesus, he has a totally different reaction from the rich young ruler. Zacchaeus didn't dare go to Jesus – he hid in a tree, hoping to just see Him, but Jesus went to him and invited Himself to dinner. Jesus didn't even mention money to Zacchaeus, but Zacchaeus decided to give half of everything he had to the poor and to repay everyone he had cheated. The moment he met Jesus, everything changed for Zacchaeus and he was ready to do the right thing for God.

Did you know?

Goats can actually climb trees. You might not see this at your local park, but if you went to Morocco you'd find goats climbing argan trees to eat the delicious berries that are similar to olives.

Something to talk about

· Have you ever hidden from anyone?
· How long did it take for someone to find you?

Bekah says...

If you met Jesus, do you think there might be something you would want to change in your life? Why not talk to Him about it now?

Pray

Dear Lord Jesus, thank You that I can never hide from You. You can always find me. I want You to change me like You changed Zacchaeus. Amen.

Hiding

Luke 22:49–53

'When the disciples who were with Jesus saw what was going to happen, they asked, "Shall we use our swords, Lord?" And one of them struck the High Priest's slave and cut off his right ear. But Jesus said, "Enough of this!" He touched the man's ear and healed him. Then Jesus said to the chief priests and the officers of the temple guard and the elders who had come there to get him, "Did you have to come with swords and clubs, as though I were an outlaw? I was with you in the Temple every day, and you did not try to arrest me. But this is your hour to act, when the power of darkness rules."'

Something to think about

In today's verses, we are coming to the end of Jesus' time on earth. It's the night before He's going to be killed on the cross, and the soldiers are coming to arrest Him. These men aren't coming because they believe Jesus is special, that He could heal them or could change their lives. They're coming because they think He's a trouble maker, but they're scared of what could happen so they come in the night, with weapons. But they don't meet a dangerous trouble maker. They meet the Son of God and even at this moment, when one of the soldiers gets wounded, Jesus reaches out and heals His enemy. How amazing. I wonder how that soldier felt after that? The Bible doesn't tell us, but it makes you realise that you can see God do amazing things and still not follow Him. One of the group gets his ear healed – yet still they arrest Jesus.

Bekah says...

We all make some bad decisions, even when we know Jesus really well. But the key is to stop and say sorry. Jesus always forgives us.

Did you know?

Harry Potter creator J.K. Rowling received 12 rejections in a row from publishers, until the eight-year-old daughter of an editor asked to read the rest of the book. The editor agreed to publish Rowling's story but advised her to get a day job as she had 'little chance' of making money in children's books. The book then went on to sell over 50 million copies.

Something to talk about

- Has there ever been a time when, despite knowing Jesus, you made a bad choice anyway?
- How did you feel afterwards?

Pray

Dear Lord Jesus, I don't ever want to ignore who You really are. Help me to follow You closely, always. Amen.

Investigate

Luke 23:1-4

'The whole group rose up and took Jesus before Pilate, where they began to accuse him: "We caught this man misleading our people, telling them not to pay taxes to the Emperor and claiming that he himself is the Messiah, a king." Pilate asked him, "Are you the king of the Jews?"

"So you say," answered Jesus. Then Pilate said to the chief priests and the crowds, "I find no reason to condemn this man."'

Something to think about

Pilate was the Roman governor of Judea. He was the top man in the area, so the Jews who arrested Jesus took Him to Pilate, so that Pilate could sentence Jesus to death. They made up a whole bunch of stories about Jesus to make Him look terrible. When Pilate met Jesus, all he knew about Him was what he had been told by these other leaders, but after talking to Jesus, he realised there was nothing bad about Him at all. He met Jesus and knew He wasn't what people said. Pilate took the time to investigate and work it out for himself. We live in a world where many people don't believe Jesus was who He said He was. It's easy to go along with the crowd, but it's worth looking at the evidence, having a proper investigation so that, like Pilate, we can discover that Jesus really is the Son of God.

Bekah says...

When our girls were in Year 7, they had to take part in a debate about whether Jesus was really who He said He was. Most of the other children argued that Jesus was a fake, but we helped our girls to discover the evidence that Jesus really rose from the dead, and it helped them to grow in confidence about Him.

Did you know?

There's a lot of evidence outside of the Bible for the existence of Jesus. Within a few decades of His life, Jesus is mentioned by Jewish and Roman historians, as well as by dozens of Christian writings. He certainly wasn't a first-century fairytale.

Something to talk about

· What convinced you that Jesus really is the Son of God?
· How can you help other people to discover who Jesus is?

Pray

Dear Lord Jesus, thank You for being real, and not a fairytale. Help me to know You and help others to know You too. Amen.

Perspective

Luke 23:39–43

'One of the criminals hanging there hurled insults at him: "Aren't you the Messiah? Save yourself and us!" The other one, however, rebuked him, saying, "Don't you fear God? You received the same sentence he did. Ours, however, is only right, because we are getting what we deserve for what we did; but he has done no wrong." And he said to Jesus, "Remember me, Jesus, when you come as King!" Jesus said to him, "I promise you that today you will be in Paradise with me."'

Something to think about

It's the last moments of Jesus' life. He's been nailed to the tree, and still there are new people for Him to meet. These two criminals have done terrible things, and now they're paying the price. But they have two very different reactions to Jesus. The first laughs at Jesus and teases Him, daring Jesus to get down from the cross. The other man sees Jesus and knows who He is. He understands that he is on the cross because he's done bad things, but that Jesus has never done anything wrong. He doesn't tease Jesus; instead he asks Jesus to remember him. Even though Jesus is dying right next to him, this man trusts that Jesus will return as the King. It doesn't make sense, but somehow he understands.

Steve says...

I joined the Boys' Brigade when I was 12 years old. We had to go to church, and although I didn't enjoy the Sunday meetings, I put up with it because we played football as a group every Saturday (and because we got to see the Girls' Brigade). It wasn't until I went on a BB camp that I first heard about Jesus in a way I could understand, and decided to follow Him. I've never looked back.

Did you know?

Experts say it takes just seven seconds to make a first impression. People decide what they think about you very quickly.

Something to talk about

· Was there a time when you met Jesus but chose not to follow Him?
· Why do you think you did this?

Bekah says...

We've talked a lot about Jesus in the pages of the book, but maybe you've not yet made a decision to trust Him. Would you like to change that today? The prayer below will help you with that first step.

Pray

Dear Lord Jesus, I want to get to know You. Here and now, I choose to trust You and follow You. Please remember me when You come as King. Amen.

The best news

Matthew 28:1–7

'After the Sabbath, as Sunday morning was dawning, Mary Magdalene and the other Mary went to look at the tomb. Suddenly there was a violent earthquake; an angel of the Lord came down from heaven, rolled the stone away, and sat on it. His appearance was like lightning, and his clothes were white as snow. The guards were so afraid that they trembled and became like dead men. The angel spoke to the women. "You must not be afraid," he said. "I know you are looking for Jesus, who was crucified. He is not here; he has been raised, just as he said. Come here and see the place where he was lying. Go quickly now, and tell his disciples, 'He has been raised from death, and now he is going to Galilee ahead of you; there you will see him!' Remember what I have told you."'

Something to think about

Some of Jesus' best friends were women, and the two Marys were very close to Him. When Jesus died on the cross, they were desperately upset. So on the Sunday, they went to sit by His grave and think about Him. What they saw when they got there was not what they expected, and it changed their lives forever. What they found wasn't a dead body, it was an empty tomb and an angel! The angel had the best news ever – Jesus was alive! – and he gave the women the most important job in the history of the world – to go and tell everyone else the good news. What an amazing day; the Marys started the day feeling sad and frightened, but finished happy and excited and full of stories.

Something to talk about

· Have you ever had a day that began sadly but ended happily?
· What changed?

Pray

Dear Jesus, thank You for changing the world for me and for everyone who follows You. Help me to share that good news with others! Amen.

Something for the weekend

Meeting Jesus is the best thing that can happen to anyone, and it's good to bring our friends to meet Him. Why not make a list of people you know who don't yet know Jesus, and, as a family, start praying for them?

Bible reading notes designed especially
for each member of the family

With six different titles available as one-year subscriptions, you and everyone in your family can be inspired on their own faith journey every day of the year. Choose your way of engaging with the Bible:

Insightful and encouraging Bible reading notes for men and women

Practical and relevant daily guidance for teenagers

Fun and engaging daily readings for children

| Every Day with Jesus | Inspiring Women Every Day | Life Every Day (Jeff Lucas) | Mettle 15–18s | YP's 11–14s | Topz 7–11s |

For more information, current prices and to order a one-year subscription, visit **cwr.org.uk/subscriptions** or call **01252 784700**.
Also available from Christian bookshops.

For young readers aged 3–6, Pens help introduce Bible reading and prayer in a colourful and accessible way.
Visit our website for more information.

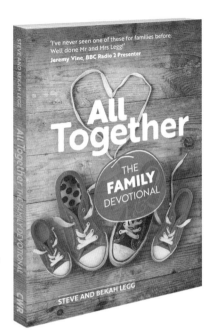

Bring your family together again!

Continue your daily, shared experience of the Bible with *All Together: The Family Devotional*

With this 12-week devotional also by Steve and Bekah Legg, discover more of the Bible together – from Creation, Moses and Esther, to the birth, life and resurrection of Jesus. Infused with Steve and Bekah's insight from their own large family, each day includes Bible readings, thoughts and questions that open up the Scriptures and spark conversation.

Authors: Steve and Bekah Legg

ISBN: 978-1-78259-692-9